No Longer in Pieces

No Longer in Pieces
An Intimate Memoir of Grace and Redemption

Jennifer R. Ward

XULON PRESS

Xulon Press Elite
2301 Lucien Way #415
Maitland, FL 32751
407.339.4217
www.xulonpress.com

Unless otherwise indicated, Scripture quotations taken from the King James Version (KJV) – *public domain.*

Scripture quotations taken from the Holy Bible, New International Version (NIV). Copyright © 1973, 1978, 1984, 2011 by Biblica, Inc.™. Used by permission. All rights reserved.

Printed in the United States of America.

ISBN-13: 978-1-63221-897-1

No Longer in Pieces is a fly-on-the-wall view of what it took for me to finally accept myself and to love myself as God sees and loves me.

Certain names and dates have been changed or withheld to protect the innocent and the not so innocent.

Please note: Some content depicts violence, controversial topics, sexual violence against a minor (which could trigger post-traumatic stress disorder), and other things that some may consider profane, vulgar, or offensive.

DEDICATION

This book is dedicated to my son Anton L. Strong Jr.,
and my mother Patricia D. Ward.
My greatest teachers of acceptance and unconditional love.

TABLE OF CONTENTS

INTRODUCTION

WRITING THIS BOOK WAS TERRIFYING. I AM stripping myself naked to show my scars and the holes. In some instances, those wounds were self-inflicted. In every instance, I hope my lessons inspire others to seek wholeness.

No Longer in Pieces is a fly-on-a-wall glimpse of the emotional and reckless turmoil I went through as a child and young woman and the losses it took for me to give God a yes.

As a young girl, I would hear an internal whisper whenever I was in a place or around people who were not good for me. Today, I recognize that whispering voice as the Holy Spirit. Back then, I did not always listen to the prompting, and I often suffered the consequences for ignoring them.

After you read my book, I hope you will get to know your own internal prompting voice as a friend. Furthermore, like me, I hope you learn that you can have healthy relationships once you become a healthier you. With that, come on this journey with me to see how I began to connect my pieces.

THE BEGINNING

MY EARLIEST MEMORY IS ARRIVING AT THE Henry Horner projects on the west side of Chicago in the mid-seventies. My mom, Patricia—who everyone called by her middle name, Diane—was holding me with her right hand and my older sister, Chandra, with her left.

The buildings were the tallest I had ever seen and looked as if they could reach the clouds in the sky. Coming from a small Mississippi town named Cruger, I found everything about Chicago was overwhelming—the speedy cars, the noisy trains, and the number of people. There were more people living in one of the project buildings than the entire population in Cruger.

We moved to Chicago because my mother's sister, Minnie Lee, had left Cruger months earlier to be with her boyfriend.

Shortly after arriving, he left her for another woman. With minimal options, my auntie moved into the Henry Horner projects. At that time, she was in her early twenties, a mother of four children, three boys and one girl. My mom moved in to help her sister with paying the bills and to take care of her children.

My mom had given birth to my sister Chandra and me around that same time. We were born two years apart, almost to the date. Chandra was born March 15, 1970, while I was born March 13, 1972. Our mom dressed us alike and took us everywhere she went. Whether we went to the store or the apartment of one of her friends in the projects, we were always with her. I say "were" because Chandra died at twenty-three years of age from an accidental overdose of medication—as noted on her death certificate.

There was a one-year difference between my mom and her sister Minnie Lee. My mother, shy and reserved, was the eldest of seven. Everyone always thought my auntie Minnie Lee was the oldest, for she was the livelier and bossier of the two sisters. I think my mom's demeanor was so quiet because she had polio as a child. She had to wear braces on her legs to keep her from falling and to assist her with walking. The leg braces were like the ones worn by the younger Forrest Gump character in the movie by the same name starring Tom Hanks. Because of my mom's polio, her ability to get around was limited, and she looked to my auntie Minnie Lee for direction and security. However, as adults their relationship was often contentious.

Maybe their tension came from having to depend on one another as young girls who were often left without much adult supervision by their mother—sometimes for days. They fought so much it is a wonder to me how they were as close as they were.

While we were living in the projects, drinking alcohol was considered a standard weekend pastime. The adults in our apartment were no different. Whenever they drank, our home would become a battle zone. The sisters would fight and call each other names. I watched my mom and auntie Minnie Lee fight in the evening and behave the next day as if nothing had happened. When the next weekend came along, all the family secrets and stories would come out when the bottles and cans were opened, starting at five p.m. on Fridays, and would not stop until early Sunday morning.

Several households in those project buildings were like mine: African American families that had migrated to Chicago from the south, headed by single mothers because fatherless homes were a requirement to be eligible for low-income apartments and monthly welfare checks. The movie *Claudine*, released in the early seventies, starred the iconic actress Diahann Carroll, who did an amazing job portraying the experiences of single black women like my mom and my auntie Minnie Lee.

My mom and aunt remained close until the day Minnie Lee died due to complications with her heart. She was sixty-five, and my mother was sixty-six. Growing up in that type of environment left us children to entertain ourselves. This allowed me to meet one of my first childhood friends in the project, a girl named Stephanie. Her family were Christians. She would invite me over to listen to Christian music and would talk to me about God. My family believed in God; however, they never took us to church. Whenever I would ask about going to church, they would say that they had gone enough times when they were kids.

Stephanie and her family did not live in the projects for a long time; they moved out within a year after they moved in. I did not mind losing Stephanie as a friend because I still had my cousins to play with.

Despite the government restrictions, my auntie Minnie Lee and my mom both had boyfriends who lived with us. My uncle Obrey went by his nickname Pookey and had two more children with my auntie Minnie Lee. Uncle Pookey was considered the man of the house, and he treated all nine children as his own.

My mother's boyfriend was named Larry. Before meeting Larry my mom had another boyfriend named John. On one hot summer day, my mom had taken Chandra and me with her to purchase a fan. While walking from the store John started talking to our mom. I was small, maybe three years old. John had a kindness about him. He'd complimented my mom on how good she was doing with my sister and me. They ended up spending a lot of time together. There was talk above our heads about marriage. My mom's fate, instead, was to meet Larry.

Between her relationships with John and Larry, my mom had my little brother Terry with a man named Spencer, who never took responsibility for my brother.

My mom was not the best at choosing men who treated her well. To be fair, Larry was not all bad. He was quite funny and hardworking. He and my mom were physically attracted to one another, but otherwise they only shared a love for family and alcohol. John tried a few times to get my mom back to no avail. "Larry had his hooks in her," or at least that was how the adults talked about it. Just like the small town of Cruger, almost everyone in the projects knew everyone else's business and spoke openly about everything, even in the presence of children.

Larry and I did not have the best father-daughter relationship from the time I was about six or seven, when I saw him slap my mother's face. He also resented my brother, because my mom got pregnant with him while they were together. My mom had been over to one of her friends who lived near the projects. She came home late that night and her shirt was on backwards. Two to three times, Larry asked her why her shirt was backwards but slapped her face before she could answer. I got up from my sleeping mat and told him not to hit my mom again.

He was mad and told my mom that I needed to apologize for "getting out of a child's place." Even at that age I had a strong sense of what was right and wrong, and I was not going to apologize to him. In my opinion, he should have been apologizing to me. Instead, he didn't speak to me for weeks. He would not even allow me to watch the television in the bedroom that he shared with my mom.

Throughout my childhood, I would stick up for my mom when she and Larry would fight whenever she did something he did not like. Either he would get mad at me or she would get mad at me. The pattern continued for twenty years until they separated, for good, in the mid-nineties. None of it ever made sense to me.

Despite the drinking and fighting, my mom and my auntie Minnie Lee felt they were good parents, since they were in the home with us and they did not leave us for weeks and months at a time as our grandmother had left them. They would often tell us, "you have a roof over your head and food in the house, don't you?" It was not until we were adults that we shared with them that we were not fine at all.

Chapter
2

APARTMENT 702

THE APARTMENT WE LIVED IN HAD TWO FLOORS, with three bedrooms and a single bathroom upstairs, a large living room and medium-sized kitchen downstairs. My mom and Larry shared one bedroom; auntie Minnie Lee and uncle Pookey shared another bedroom; nine of us children shared the largest bedroom. It may sound odd that so many people lived in such a tiny apartment in the projects, but that was normal. We had some great times in that apartment.

We often played outside on the ramps with other kids in our building. The girls would jump rope, play house, or do each other's hair. The boys would play with stray dogs in the area, shoot basketball, or play marbles. We could stay outside all day if we wanted to, until dinner or the streetlights came on.

Dett elementary school was a few blocks from our project building, and my cousins and I would walk to and from school each weekday together. This journey was our routine during the week, and on the weekends, we were to stay out of the adults' way.

Typical of many weekend nights in my family's apartment, it was full of people. Their weekends were for the adults to drink alcohol, smoke marijuana, and hang out with their friends playing card games. The adults were mainly downstairs and came upstairs just to use the only bathroom in the apartment. We children were either outside playing on the ramp or upstairs in our room playing with each other.

On this night, I must have been between the ages of three and four years old. I was still wearing my starter panties. I had been with my mom earlier that night on the ninth floor of the building. My mom was visiting with Larry's mom, Ms. Mary, and I'd fallen asleep in my mom's lap. My mom decided to take me downstairs to our apartment on the seventh floor and put me to bed. I can only assume that my mom put me in her bed because she presumed no one would wake me. Unfortunately, she didn't know everyone in the apartment that night.

I woke up to one of my older "play" cousins pulling down my panties. He was the son of a friend of auntie Minnie Lee and my mom who lived in a neighboring building. He put something slick between my legs, like Vaseline. Then he put his penis inside of me, slowly. I wasn't sure what he was doing to me, but I felt it was wrong. I knew I was scared. I pretended that I was not awake. I was terrified to make any sound.

He began to move up and down on me. A few times or a thousand—I don't remember. The bedroom door was cracked open so he could see if someone was coming up the stairs. He stopped once he heard someone in the hallway. It was my uncle Pookey. He came upstairs, went in and out of his and my auntie Minnie Lee's bedroom, and went back down the stairs. He never looked in my mom's bedroom. If he had come a few minutes earlier, my uncle might have interrupted the event that forever changed me and how I saw men. I also resented my mom and my sister for years for not being there to save me.

I never told anyone about what happened to me, mainly because I didn't have the language. I would not have the words until I learned about sex in the sixth grade. In a flood of memory, I felt ashamed and embarrassed about what he did to me. He laid his body on top of mine when he heard my uncle coming up the stairs, trying to cover me up. When uncle Pookey headed down the stairs, the boy removed his penis from inside of me and pulled my panties back up. He slid from the bed onto the floor, then crept out of the room.

Once I felt that he had gone away, I rolled off the bed and onto the floor too. I did the only thing I knew, which was to make my way back to my mom. I padded back to the ninth floor and pulled myself into her lap. It would be years before I spoke about that night.

Being silent and suppressing my memories didn't keep me from feeling ashamed. Even though my intellect knows I did nothing wrong, because that molestation happened to me, I warred within myself for decades. The episode is still unresolved; our families are still close. Admittedly, avoidance is still my tool of choice towards the person who molested me. I have visualized myself confronting him. I saw myself asking why he did that to me? To any child? I pray the courage will find me one day.

THE TEEN YEARS

MY FAMILY DYNAMIC CAUSED ME TO GROW UP feeling isolated and broken. I carried a sense of emptiness that took many years to identify and even more to reconcile.

In my formative years, I escaped my feelings of loneliness through my imagination. I created dream worlds of my future life, letting my mind explore there instead of the realities outside of my closed eyes. One of my favorite games to play was house. I fantasized about getting married and having three to four children with my one and only husband.

I say my one and only husband because my mother and many of the women in my neighborhood had children by different men. I knew that I did not want to be like "those women." My plan was to do the opposite of what my mom did. I would eventually come to realize how ignorant my judgement was, especially of my own mother. I would come to understand that only God knows our journey's roadmap.

My grandmother's name was Rosetta, but everyone knew her as "Honey Punch." I lovingly called her husband Papa. When I would visit Grandma Honey in the summers, Papa and I would sit on the porch and talk for hours. He made me laugh with stories about the people in Cruger. I would miss his stories when I had to go back home to Chicago.

None of Grandma Honey's children were Papa's biological children. Regardless of that fact, he was still one of my favorite persons in the world. He was an old, skinny Native American man of average height with long thin grey hair and a small pot belly. I learned years later that Papa would beat my grandmother whenever he was drunk.

I had never witnessed Papa beat my grandmother. Of course, they were both elderly when I visited them and they no longer fought as they did when my mom and her siblings were younger. I noticed scars on her body as a child, but I didn't dare ask about them. They looked like healed cut wounds.

There were also stories that Papa had molested my aunties and my mom when they were young girls. I did not learn the news about Papa until after he died. Hearing that news was devastating to me, because I loved Papa very much. Just as horrifying, the news made me look at Papa's interactions with me as a child differently: Was he really only giving me money when I was a child so I could have some ice cream or was he just grooming me so he could do the same thing to me that he had done to my aunties and my mom?

I am not sure how I would have reacted to him if he was still alive. I'm grateful that he never touched me in any way that made me feel uncomfortable. In fact, each time I was with him I only felt the love of a grandfather from him. Unfortunately, Papa was like the other serious topics in my family that should have been addressed in a sober and rational matter, and out of the ear shot of children. Ultimately, the stories collected from the adults in my family left me feeling perplexed. I never knew the ratio of exaggeration to truth in a story or how much was based upon facts or fiction.

One day, out of the blue, my mother announced that my sister and I were going to live with Grandma Honey. My sister was going because her biological father—who I affectionately came to call Pops— needed help around the house. He was ailing, and his wife had worsening arthritis. Chandra traveled a few months before me. I went right before the school semester was to start in Mississippi. I did not want to go to Cruger, but the move was not up for discussion. We were supposed to return to Chicago after a year.

Several years before I moved back to Mississippi, Papa had died and the house he lived in with my grandmother had burned down. By the time I moved there, my grandmother and my auntie Elizabeth had purchased two separate trailers on the property. Because my auntie Elizabeth lived so close, my grandmother was able to help my auntie with her kids. With two small children to mind, I knew they couldn't afford the fancy things a teenage girl would want, and I dared not ask.

My sister Chandra liked living there more than I did, mainly because Pops was able to offer her more than our mom ever did when we lived in Chicago. Instead of being third in line of nine children, she was now the oldest of four siblings in Cruger. Pop's wife, Irene, appreciated having Chandra around to help with cleaning and maintaining their home. She sewed clothes for my sister and her siblings. I was able to wear the clothes that Irene sewed for Chandra when I would hang out with my sister at their house.

The highlight of my week was on Thursday nights. On those evenings I got to spend time with my sister at Pop's house. I would try on her clothes and watch the Cosby show. I was not able to watch the Cosby show at the trailers of my grandmother or my auntie Elizabeth because they didn't have an antenna for all the channels. Auntie Elizabeth would get mad about the amount of time I spent over Pop's house. If I stayed past nine o'clock, she would walk across the dirt road to get me. I never understood why she got so upset. She knew where I was the entire time. Ultimately, she got tired of having to come to get me, and they purchased the equipment so that I could watch the Cosby show at home.

I mainly hung out with my grandmother and walked the neighborhood with her as she visited with her friends in town. Periodically, she let me ride with her to the department stores or restaurants in Greenwood. I would travel with Chandra and

Pops to visit his family in Greenwood too or go to church in Tchula. I liked how the people spoke to you even if they did not know your name. It was bizarre at first, but then I learned to expect that everyone you came across would wave and say hello to you, even if they did not know you.

I hadn't met any cute boys in Cruger who weren't either relatives or too old for me. I wasn't disappointed, because I knew I would be going back to Chicago once the school year ended. Other than watching television to pass time, I listened to the radio. The local stations played mostly country music. After a while, I started to enjoy country artists like Garth Brooks and the Judds.

I hated living in Cruger. I missed my family and friends. The kids in the neighborhood spoke funny to my ears, and they made fun of my ghetto slang when I used words like "homey." A girl at my new school bullied me. She would talk about my hair and clothes. I couldn't understand why she would bully me when she looked exactly like me. I didn't have anything, and neither did she. Yet she stressed me incessantly. One day I noticed a red stain on the back of her pants and told her. She went with our teacher into the bathroom. When she returned, she told me that her period had just started. We didn't become best friends, like in the movies, but she was nicer to me after that.

I saw my biological father one time. A childhood friend of my mom's, Annie Mae, asked if I wanted to meet my father. I only knew his name: Alonso Banks. When I was seven or eight, my mom said she wanted me to know who my father was. She told me his name, and I'd never forgotten it.

Grandma Honey didn't want me to start any trouble. Despite her apprehension, I wanted to meet my father. Annie Mae took me by the hand and pulled me towards the house where my father was visiting. A boy who went to my school was standing in the yard, however, and I chickened out.

He was standing right next to my father, with his brother and a couple other men. They were all having a conversation that I was too far away to hear. I paused and stood there on the dirt road, immediately telling Annie Mae, " I change my mind."

I changed my mind because I didn't want that boy to tell everyone at school that I didn't know who my father was. I realized, later, that the boy was probably my cousin. So I missed a chance to meet my father and get to know some of my extended family.

I regret not meeting my biological father. Fear of what others might think of me got the best of me. It wouldn't be the last time I allowed fear of others to block me from an opportunity.

I often thought about looking for my biological father, but ultimately decided against it. He was married when he got my mother pregnant—at least that's the story I heard retold over the years. Year after year, I would decide that I'd waited too long. After some time, I'd even convinced myself that it wasn't that important.

I also rationalized that someone else might have minimized the importance. A betting person could wager that my biological father had family members who knew that I existed. For one, he had an aunt named Ms. Mary Thomas who lived across the road from my grandmother. Ms. Thomas owned the local candy store in Cruger. She sold the best ice cream I had ever tasted, and she was always kind to me whenever I returned to Cruger to visit my grandmother.

As soon as the school year came to an end, I begged my grandmother to send me back home. I did not want to wait until the end of summer. I was ready to go as soon as humanly possible. My grandmother did not want me to leave her, but she knew how much I missed my family and friends, so she agreed to send me back home to Chicago.

When I returned home to Chicago in the summer of 1986, the entire environment had changed. We no longer lived in the projects. My mom and my auntie Minnie Lee no longer lived together in the same apartment. I moved in with my mom, Larry, and my little brother, Terry. We lived in a basement apartment of a duplex home on the west side of Chicago. Auntie Minnie Lee and uncle Pookey lived further west with my six cousins. Living there, I felt poorer than I had living in the projects. I could not believe that all we could afford was a basement that was converted into an apartment.

On my first night back at home, I went to auntie Minnie Lee's house instead of staying with my mom. My cousin Sammie called me up to his room to let me know what had gone down while I was away in Mississippi. He told me how auntie Minnie Lee had lost the apartment in the projects because my mom and Larry had gotten into a fight. He'd spat in my mom's face, which triggered something in her. She grabbed a knife and stabbed Larry in the face, barely missing his temple, which would have killed him instantly.

Sammie said my mom was the one who called the police and met them as they pulled up to the building. My mom told them what she had done and why. Larry did not press charges, so my mother never went to jail for stabbing him.

After that drama, my mom moved to one side of town and my auntie Minnie Lee moved to a different side. Their duplex allowed for cousins Sammie and Johnnie to share the attic and turn it into their own little apartment. My cousin Chris mainly hung out with his friends. Falesia and I went back to hanging out like we did before I left for Mississippi. We would pretty much hang around the house playing. When we got annoyed with each other we would fight, or I would just go home to my mother's apartment. My cousins Pooh and Peaches, as well as my little brother Terry, were the youngest, so they would just hang out with each other.

Once school started, I pretty much lived with my mom during the week and hung out with my cousins on the weekend. This pattern continued until I became friends with my classmate Corinn at my new elementary school Tilton.

Tilton Elementary was less than a mile from my home, so I would walk to and from school by myself. I was in eighth grade that year when I met Corinn. I also met Lamont. He was best friends with Corinn's boyfriend Trent.

Lamont and I were in separate eighth grade homerooms. My homeroom teacher once had me deliver a note to Lamont's homeroom teacher, and according to Corinn, Lamont had leaned over to Trent to ask him who I was. Not too long after, Corinn and I started hanging out with the two of them after school from time to time. Some of the boys and girls in school were already having sex. I had never been kissed by a boy; I didn't want to have sex yet, but I did like hanging out with Lamont.

I liked Lamont a lot, but more than that, I really liked his family, and they liked me too. His dad would tease Lamont by saying, "Why does such a pretty girl like your big-head self?" I liked Lamont because he reminded me of everything I was not: he was whole, was sure of himself, knew what he liked and what he didn't, and didn't let anyone change his mind, not even me.

In the middle of our eighth-grade year, the four of us were sitting outside the empty school just before sunset atop of concrete blocks. Corinn and Trent were kissing on one side in the front of the building. Lamont and I were across on a separate concrete block. It was my first kiss, and it was everything. His lips were soft as he pulled me close to him. I felt good all over my entire body. I don't remember how the conversation happened, but Lamont and I were talking about having sex only a few weeks after that kiss. We would go to Trent's house—his mom wouldn't be home. Corinn and Trent would be alone in one room, and Lamont and I would be alone in another. Corinn and I walked to Trent's house with nervousness and excitement. His mother would be playing cards at her sister's house, leaving us plenty of time to do the do.

I blurted out, "My mom would kill me if she found out what I was about to do!" Trent calmly responded by saying, "Then don't tell her." He'd met us along the walk. We all laughed at how naïve I was as we trekked to Trent's house. To our disappointment, not only was Trent's mom home, but it was her week to host the card game, so the house was full of people.

Not long after our first brilliant plan failed, I got invited to spend the night by Lamont's older sister, Sharon. Of course, I jumped at the chance to be in the same space as Lamont. I was so giddy because I knew we would have sex that night. Sharon had taken me under her wing as a god daughter, and I was able to talk with her about anything. That night, all I wanted to talk about was Lamont. I'd also developed a crush on Corinn's older brother Nookie. They both had qualities that I wished the other had. I looked at Lamont as my puppy-dog kind of love and Nookie as the bad-boy I was drawn to.

I had no way of knowing that Lamont was listening the entire time on the other side of Sharon's door. He heard me telling Sharon that I liked them both but liked Lamont more. He heard me say I didn't think Lamont liked me as much as I liked him. In comparison, I said, Nookie made me feel like I was the best person he'd ever met. In the middle of my talking,

Lamont exploded into the room, laughing at me. I started reaching for anything to throw at him, to shut up his taunting laughs. The last item I threw flew past his head when he ducked and into the display of basketball awards in the living room, breaking one of his trophies in half.

I gasp! As Sharon declared, "he shouldn't have been snooping." Lamont ended up messing up the night for both of us. I had hoped he would come and get me from Sharon's room so we could fool around, but he never did. He didn't speak to me again for days. We never moved past second base and never discussed that night again.

All the time while we were boyfriend and girlfriend, Lamont and I would argue often. It mostly had to do with me, because I would be dishonest with him about some of the simplest of things. When he insisted on seeing where I lived, I lied and told him that our family owned the building and only lived in the basement because there were not that many of us. Lamont would be critical of me whenever he caught me lying. I would get emotional, which led to break-ups off and on throughout middle and high school.

By the time we were fourteen years old, we were beginning to follow different paths. We were already opposites in many ways. Lamont grew up in a two-parent household with many brothers and sisters, while I was a girl from the projects living in a basement apartment with my brother, mother, and her live-in boyfriend Larry. We shared some of the same friends in school, but Lamont would not hang out with us on weekends.

On Friday nights, my friends and I would pay an older person hanging outside the liquor store to purchase beer and wine for us to drink. Some of the kids would drink and others would smoke weed. Lamont did not participate in either activity, at least not around me.

One night, I got so drunk while at the house of one of the neighborhood kids that I needed Corinn and our friend Crystal to carry me home. Drinking made me feel less shy.

Despite having a social circle and a boyfriend, I was often uncomfortable around crowds of people. As I reflect, I'm sure I felt intimidation from crowds because I had been molested. For me to feel comfortable around anyone, I would had to have known that person or feel at peace around them, especially when it came to boys or men. Drinking also pushed back waves of sorrow I found more and more difficult to dismiss.

On Saturdays, we went to the roller rink. I would just hang around the wall waiting for the DJ to play a slow song—I enjoyed rhythm and blues (R&B) music. If I'd get asked to dance, I ended up saying "no," because I only wanted to dance with Lamont. I begged him several times to come to the rink so we could hang out. He would say that he was not a dancer or that he did not like the rink, and he never came.

He told me no so many times that I eventually stopped asking him. One night, someone from a dance crew asked me to dance—he was the older cousin of my friend Crystal. I said yes. He raised my hands to loop them around his neck and shoulders. He put his hands around my waist and then started rubbing my hips and butt. I wrote in my diary about how I'd never had anyone rub my butt like that before. Little did I know that little message in my pocket-size diary would come back to haunt me.

I didn't want my little brother finding my diary and telling our mother everything he learned. It turns out the diary was less secure with me at school. Without knowing it, I dropped it in a classroom, and someone handed the diary over to my teacher. Within the cover of the diary, it said "Jennifer loves Lamont" with a heart around our names. Instead of pulling me aside, she read my diary out loud to the entire classroom. When I wrote about the boy rubbing my butt, everyone thought I was talking about Lamont. I never claimed the diary, and I denied it every time someone asked me about it. There was another Jennifer in my homeroom, so I allowed everyone to think that the diary might belong to her. When Lamont told me that he knew the diary was mine, I still denied it. We broke up soon afterwards.

We remained friendly but rarely spoke to one another. After we moved on to two different high schools during the next academic year, we did not make any effort to spend time together. When Lamont no longer showed interest in me, I gave all my time to Nookie. I would hang out with Corinn, letting Nookie hug and kiss me. Nookie had my mind blown. I believed everything he said to me, even in the face of evidence that showed he was lying to me. One Christmas he brought me a nice long red coat. I was so happy to receive that coat until I found out that he and his friends had stolen coats from a warehouse, and I was one of four girls to get the same coat.

I couldn't shake him. Nookie was the first boy I had sex with. At least that is how I rationalized the foolishness in my head. One time, he told me to come to his house with him so he could talk with me. I was barely in the house before we were on his bed kissing. I told him no as he started to unbutton my pants, yet he kept trying to take them down. I told him no again. When I tried to get up, he bit me on the chin. As I refused, his bite got more intense until I allowed him to take off my pants. I did not move or say anything while he had sex with me. I was stunned. He walked me home afterwards, as if he had not just forced himself on me.

Instead of avoiding Nookie, I would allow him to take me to different places so we could have sex. He told me that he loved me and that he had plans for us to be together forever. I allowed him to do whatever he wanted to do to me. He would teach me how to move and roll my body in ways that would make him feel good. He had me thinking that because we were having sex, I belonged to him. He would check on me after school, and he would call to make sure that I was at home when I said I would be. If I ever did anything that he did not like, he would slap me across my face.

I knew Nookie was not good for me. I stayed because I believed that once you had sex with a man, you were united in some pseudo-religious teenager understanding of religion. Moreover, because I witnessed my mom being abused by men,

I believed a man only hit you because he loves you so much. I believed this to be true about Nookie, because when I had shared with him that I had been molested as a child, he declared (even though he abused me) that he would kill anyone that ever put their hands on me. He said I should never show him the person who molested me, because he would hurt him. I never considered how twisted his logic was.

I would try to stay away from him and talk to other boys, but he would threaten the other boys in my high school to stay away from me. One time, I was hanging out at the house of a boy who was a classmate of mine. Suddenly there was a knock at the door. As my friend opened the door, Nookie burst into the apartment and snatched me up from the boy's bed by my hair. He pulled me by my hand through the front door. He came with what seemed like the entire block from our neighborhood. When he got me to the top of the stairs, he hit me so hard that he knocked me out for a few seconds.

Nookie pulled me to the street where the boy and everyone else had followed us. The boy asked me who I wanted to be with between the two of them. When I looked at Nookie, he glared a threat like "I wish you would say the other boy's name..." I said that I just wanted to go home. Instead, Nookie took me with him. We ended up at one of the spots where he sold drugs, and he began scolding me as if I was his child. He kept barking that he came there to save me from that boy and his brother running a train on me. None of that was true. He just lost his mind when he thought that I was going to have sex with someone else.

My friends and a few of my girl cousins knew that Nookie was abusing me. He would hit me anytime he thought that I was being flip. I figured we were both following our scripts. I grew up watching my mom being abused by her partner. Nookie must have had the same unfortunate notes. Anytime someone would try to mention what Nookie was doing to my mom, aunts, or Larry, I would deny it. I knew I wanted something different but didn't know who could free me or how I could escape.

My saving grace was that Nookie ended up going to jail. After he went to jail, I was able to focus more on school. I was even able to get a part-time job while still in high school. One day I had a break from work, and I walked over to Lamont's house to see how he and his family were doing. Lamont and I were always able to talk about anything; he did not care if it hurt my feelings or not. He would always be brutally honest with me.

Once I got to his house, he and I walked to the church that was on the corner of the block. We talked about how things had been over the last couple years. He asked me if I was still a virgin, and I told him that I was not, and for some reason, I shared with him how it had happened. "Jennifer, that dude raped you," he said to me. I must have looked perplexed because he repeated it: "He raped you."

Was Lamont, right? Did Nookie rape me? I didn't know it could be rape when you knew the person. It took Lamont telling me that because Nookie had forced himself on me after I told him no, that was rape. It took a moment to really sink in. Years of moments, to be honest.

Lamont and I would not speak again for another couple of years. I would have other relationships that would only last a few months at the most. Anytime a boy started to get close to me or anytime he showed violent tendencies, I would break up with him and avoid his calls. Soon I stopped hanging around the old neighborhood and mainly just went to school and worked.

Another one of my cousins, Nickey, lived with her mom, Erma, and five brothers in a multilevel apartment building around the corner from our basement apartment. Whenever I didn't spend time with my friends from school, I hung out with Nickey. Because all my other cousins were moving away, I was grateful that I had Nickey to hang out with. We would sing, watch videos, and practice dance moves on most weekends. We were like peas in a pod for years. Whenever our moms would hang at each other's house, we would sit around and talk.

Some nights we would make plans to sneak out to meet up with some boys. I had her walk to Lamont's house with me one day, and right before we got to his house one of her older brothers called us and made us get into his car. He told us we better be glad he did not catch us with any boys, because he was going to beat them up. I thanked God that Lamont had not walked out his house.

Whenever I was not hanging out with Nickey, I was working at Kentucky Fried Chicken (KFC). I had been working at KFC for about a year when one of the boys I worked with said he had a friend that he wanted me to meet. Anyways, I had not had a boyfriend for a while, so I told him it would be fine for me to meet him. I did not like this boy, so I do not know why I agreed to meet his friend. I figured I would let his friend down gently and then go on about my merry way.

His friend's name was Anton. He met me after work on a Friday. We sat at one of the booths and talked. He was cute, and shy. We liked each other right away. If I wasn't at KFC, Anton would meet me at my mom's house. When I got home on a Friday after work, Anton would already be there waiting for me. He spent weekends with me and my family, playing cards and hanging out with my family's friends. For the most part Anton and I would just hang out in my room, which I shared with my brother Terry.

We got to hang out all night until early Saturday mornings. My mom and Larry, hungover, would forget he was there. Before evening, they would tell Anton it was time for him to go home, but I would tell him not to leave. We continued like this for months. It never dawned on me that Anton never talked about school, work, or his future. This was kind of normal for teenage boys in my neighborhood in the early nighties, because most of them did not expect to live past twenty-five years old.

Hanging out with Anton during the summer was cool, but school was going to start again soon, and I had plans. This was going to be my senior year, and I was finally going to be able to flex. I had a job that was paying decent money for a teenager. I bought my own clothes and did not have to rely on my mom to buy things for me. When my senior year started, I was ready with my stonewashed denim short skirt and matching denim jacket. I went to every class because I wanted everyone to see me. I was no longer the poor girl from the projects.

I did well in my classes, and my English teacher took an interest in my work. He said he enjoyed reading my papers. I enjoyed going to school and was looking forward to everything that being a senior had to offer. I wanted to go to all the games and the prom, and I had a cute boyfriend to share those experiences with!

Anton did not get excited about much. As a teenager, I never demanded much from him. We went to different high schools, so we got to spend time together only on the weekends. After a while, I started to get tired and missed a lot of days from school. My English teacher called me to see how I was doing and to find out why I had missed so many of his classes. I told him that I wasn't feeling well and that my mom was going to take me to the doctor to find out what was wrong with me. He told me to keep him informed and to let him know if he could be of any help.

Once my mom took me to the doctor, I found out I was two months pregnant. I was stunned, but not surprised. I had not been taking any birth control and had missed my period. I was irresponsible—somehow, I did not think it would happen to me. I told Anton right away that I was pregnant. He was happy and proud of himself, but I was devastated. The plans I had for my senior year came to a screeching halt. Ashamed and confused, I felt as though my life was falling apart around me, while everyone else looked at my pregnancy as some sort of rite of passage.

I knew I would be a mother someday, but I did not want it as a teenager. I did not know how it was going to come together. I wanted to be married. I wanted my children to have the same father—that dream was now dead. Anton was nice; however, he was just as damaged as I was—he never got over his parent's divorce. There was no way I was going to be with him forever, and by the time I realized that he was not the person for me, I was carrying his baby. I was feeling stuck and thought I was no different than any other girl from my neighborhood.

About three to four months into my pregnancy, Lamont came to visit me at my house. I was lying on my bed with a bunch of blankets on me. He sat across from me on my brother Terry's bed. Lamont had come to ask me to go with him to his senior prom. I was shocked that out of all the girls he could have asked, he wanted to take me. I paused, inhaled, exhaled deeply, and then I told him I couldn't go because I was pregnant.

I could literally feel our hearts breaking at that moment. Deep down, I hoped that he liked me enough to still want to take me to his prom. But I knew it was too much to expect a popular high school senior athlete to take a girl pregnant with someone else's baby to the prom, no matter how much he liked me.

Chapter

4

MOTHERHOOD/ BROKEN PROMISES

IT WAS FIVE O'CLOCK IN THE MORNING, AND I was at the end of my third trimester. I'd spent the entire night tossing and turning in bed. Every ten minutes I awoke with sharp pain in my right side and a need to urinate. The pains started coming every five minutes, then every two. The pain got so intense that I could no longer continue lying down in my bed. I got up, heard a small pop between my legs, then water came rushing down my legs.

I waddled to my mother's bedroom, where I told her my water just broke. Before we left, I called Anton to let him know I was about to have the baby. He lived about three miles from me and didn't have a car, yet he made it to the hospital quicker than us.

During the examination three different doctors checked to see the position of the baby, then they prepared me to push. The nurse talked me through each push. After I pushed three different times, AJ came out screaming with the most powerful lungs I ever heard. While I was having our baby, Anton stood outside of the room watching through a small window in the door.

I'm not sure if the medical staff insisted that Anton wait outside of the room because we were not married or if he chose to wait outside the delivery room, but that image symbolized our relationship from that day forward.

I was exhausted from pushing out AJ and passed out shortly after seeing him. I woke up four hours later. Yep, I was someone's mother. I was AJ's mother. I knew instantly that I loved him and that protecting that little person was my new responsibility. I also knew that I didn't have a clue what to do.

I was shocked that at nineteen years old I was able to leave the hospital with no vital information about caring for a baby. I was told to follow up with my doctor in a few weeks. During those weeks after I had my son, I was in disbelief of the undertaking of raising a baby. My mom and Larry were extremely happy to have a grandson. Terry, on the other hand, didn't like that he was no longer the baby in the family. I spent my days feeding and hugging AJ every second he was awake. So little else made sense anymore. I narrowed my attention to AJ and working. Even when nothing around me felt like home, I wanted to do whatever I needed to take care of my son and myself.

My plan was to get back to school and work as soon as possible. I did not wait the recommended six weeks before returning to work but went back to work at KFC only five weeks after having my son. I wanted to start earning money again as quickly as possible. I didn't want to have to borrow money from anyone.

By that time, my auntie Minnie Lee and uncle Pookey had moved their family from Chicago to Milwaukee, Wisconsin. Uncle Pookey could not keep a job in Chicago, and they thought they would have better opportunities in Milwaukee. My mom babysat AJ while I worked and returned to finish my final year of high school. I took only the classes needed to receive my diploma. I no longer had an interest in participating in any extra-curricular activities in high school—it all seemed trivial compared to the responsibilities of raising my son.

Fortunate for me, my mother enjoyed watching AJ, regardless of the amount of time I had to be away. For that, I will forever be grateful.

My son was formally named after his father, Anton Strong, Jr. His nickname, AJ, was also the initials of his parents, Anton and Jennifer. That's what I'd decided it meant for me, anyway.

Anton was proud to have a son. However, like me, he was clueless about how to raise our son. I hoped that the two of us would rise to the occasion, if not for ourselves, at least for our son. Every time Anton came up short of my expectations,

I was critical of him—showing little to no grace, even though he was a teenage father. In truth, I resented that Anton was my son's father instead of Lamont.

Unlike Anton, I grew up quickly. Taking care of AJ started to become naturally to me. When I came home from school one day, AJ could not get to me fast enough. He was walking on his tiptoes. I noticed right away a distressed look in my son's face. I scooped him up, took off the shoes he was wearing, and threw them across the room where Anton was sitting with one of his friends. He cared more about showing off the Nikes than caring for his son. If he hadn't, he would've noticed the pain on AJ's face.

I literally had to inform Anton that AJ was not moving in his walker because the shoes he put on him were too small.

While raising AJ, I had hoped that Anton would step up to be the father I needed him to be for our son, especially since neither of us had a relationship with our biological fathers. Instead, Anton pretty much left everything up to me to manage when it came to our son and relationship.

However, one-night Anton was my hero. I had been disturbed by two people arguing in our apartment who were not Larry and my mom. I realized it was a friend of Larry's who was also named Larry and the landlord's daughter. She accused Larry's friend of raping her. Hearing that, I quickly jumped out of my bed, grabbed AJ, stuffed everything I could carry into a black garbage bag, and took a cab to Anton's house. While waiting for the cab, I overheard the woman accuse Larry's friend of following her into the laundry room where she said he assaulted her. She raged outside the apartment building as Larry's friend accused her of lying about him. She then began shattering the windows of our basement apartment.

Anton lived with his mom less than ten minutes from my mom's apartment. I kept my emotions together until I reached him. He was asleep in his bedroom. I touched his shoulder. When he turned around, my eyes filled with tears. He got up quickly and asked what was wrong. I told him what happened at my mother's house and that there was no way AJ and I would go back there. He asked his mom if AJ and I could stay for a little while, and she allowed us to stay for almost two years. She told me that as long as she had a place, AJ and I would always have a place to stay.

Anton's mother and I worked, but he did not. While we were working, Anton would stay home to take care of AJ. After a while, I wanted to have our own apartment. Anton finally got a job at KFC, though he worked at a different one than I did. After he had been working for a few weeks, I decided to visit him at his job to see how things were going. Once I was there, his manager told me that Anton had quit the job a week earlier. I was surprised by that news because he would get dressed every day like he was going to work. When I confronted him about quitting his job, Anton said he was not cut out to do that type of work. I told him that he needed to do better. I did not want to raise our son alone.

Instead of getting a legal job, Anton started selling drugs, but he wasn't good at it. A few months after he'd started, he got arrested. He called his mother to inform her that he was in jail, then she gave the phone to me. He apologized for getting arrested and promised he would do better by AJ and me when he got back home.

He landed eighteen months in jail. He asked if I would wait for him. I said yes, foolishly. After Anton was in jail a few months, I reconnected with Lamont. I wanted to escape from the reality that my son's father was in jail. I decided I needed to see my friend, because I knew Lamont was a good and responsible man—he never would have made the irresponsible decision to sell drugs.

Lamont was home, visiting from college. We made plans to visit at his family's home, where he would meet AJ. When AJ and I arrived, it was as if nothing had changed between Lamont and me. Yes, I now had a child, but our connection and conversation were still easy. He liked AJ right away, and AJ liked Lamont's family dog. As I visited, Lamont would playfully call AJ his son. Lamont's dad would say AJ's father was going to kill us both. I did not tell Lamont or his family that Anton was in jail.

Lamont and I would talk over the phone. Even though he knew I lived with Anton, he would tell me to stay faithful to him. What he meant was that I should not have sex with Anton, which was not a problem, since Anton was in jail.

I never visited Anton while he was in jail. He never asked me to visit him, either. He was sent too far away, and I did not have a car at that time. We would talk often over the phone, but I never told Anton that I had started seeing Lamont again. He was in jail, and I did not want to add any additional stress on him if I didn't need to. He didn't ask me to visit, because he also didn't want to add stress on me. He knew I had a lot to do because I was taking care of our son. I appreciated that from him very much.

Whenever I had free time, I would hang out with Lamont. One night, my mom kept AJ, and I was over Lamont's house with him and his family. I had dinner with them, then afterwards Lamont and I hung out in their living room. His parent's dining and living room had nice thick carpeting on the floors. The carpet was so comfortable that Lamont and I would lie next to each other on it. Then the later in the evening it got the closer we got next to each other. His favorite thing was to ask me if I wanted a back massage; I always said yes.

While he was massaging my back, we started kissing. The next thing I knew we were in his room on his bed naked. After what seemed like forever, Lamont and I finally had sex. He pulled me close to him, and I melting into him. He lifted me off his bed and put himself inside of me as deeply as his penis could reach. I'm sure I was breathing; however, I felt as though I could not inhale and exhale. Afterwards I could not stop myself from smiling. I told him I knew we were going to eventually have sex one day. Lamont looked at me as if he was thinking, "There she goes again with her fancy world, not just enjoying the moment."

We finished loving on each other, then he and I went back to the living room. I got ready to leave to pick up AJ from my mother's house. Lamont called me once he knew I had made it home and asked me out to the movies on Friday. We went to see *Boomerang*, starring Eddie Murphy, Halle Berry, and Robin Givens. I enjoyed the movie and talking about it with Lamont until he kept saying how beautiful Halle Berry was. We argued all the way home. He was annoyed with me, saying I was being ridiculous, acting as if he had "a shot" with Halle Berry. I was annoyed because he was missing my entire point. Of course he didn't have a shot, but why spend our date talking about another woman? I thought he had intentionally started an argument with me before he had to go back to school. As our night ended, I told him to take me home.

My relationship with Lamont was confusing to me. I never took it too seriously, because he acted as though we were just friends who liked to hang out together. On the other hand, he would make grand moves that would let me know that he really did care for me. He had given me a diamond ring before he left for college after high school. It was not an engagement ring; it was more like a promise ring—a promise that we would always be friends. I'd worn that ring every day since through every relationship, including the one with Anton.

Lamont and I finally parted ways when I learned that he had married someone else soon after finishing college. He moved to Hawaii and began having his own children.

Shortly after our date, Lamont had gone back to college, with us losing connection forever. Anton was still in jail, and I knew I did not have a man to depend on—I hoped that would soon change. It was clear to me that I did not want to work at KFC my entire life. I wanted a job where I could make enough money to provide for AJ everything that I did not have when I was a child. I did not have the money to go to college, so I decided I would participate in a program that was offered for young mothers that helped us to find better-paying jobs and ultimately prepare us to have careers with better benefits and future growth. Nickey and I participated in the program together. She was also working at KFC with me.

While I was working at KFC, a guy named Andre worked there as well. He was handsome and tall. I was attracted to him for the oddest of reasons. I thought he had a nice smile and great calves. Andre was tall enough that he could have played in the NBA. All his family members that I met were also tall. When Andre and I started talking to each other, he let me know that he had a girlfriend who was pregnant with his baby. After I told him that we could not be together while he had a girlfriend, Andre broke up with his pregnant girlfriend. Sadly, I was elated instead of seeing Andre's actions as an awful character flaw. It was not one of my finest moments.

His pregnant girlfriend was clear about both of our flaws and came to KFC one night to tell me about myself and to beat me up. Thank goodness the restaurant doors were already locked when she showed up. We yelled at each other through the glass doors. I repeatedly said to her, "I am not about to fight you over Andre." She eventually left, and I never heard from or saw her again.

Andre and I continued to see each other, and word eventually got to Anton in jail. He and Andre had the same circle of friends from the neighborhood. Anton called from jail to tell me to stop seeing "dude" and called me "bogus" for not waiting on him as I'd promised. I told Anton I would not stop seeing Andre and that he was wrong to have asked me to wait in the first place. I was too young to have been put into such a situation. He again said that I was bogus, and he compared himself to Dr. Martin L. King Jr. and Malcolm X. If it was not so sad, I would have laughed at him. Instead I told him that he was no Dr. King or Malcolm X. He had gone to jail for selling drugs, not for helping anyone except himself, and he did not even do that right.

Andre and I ignored anyone's thoughts about how we were carrying on. After work, we would take a cab or get a ride from our store manager to a local motel so we could spend the night together. I was still living with Anton's mom, and I never shared with her that I was seeing someone else while Anton was in jail. No mother would've been cool with my behavior, and I did not want to take the chance that she would kick me out.

The store manager warned us to not ask him for a ride to the motel again, because he was a Christian and what we were doing went against his values. He was being a hypocrite, because he was having sex with his girlfriend even though they were not married either.

Andre and I liked having sex together. He was the first and only guy who showed me the pillow move. The move involved him stacking two pillows on top of one another and then having me lie on top of the pillows. This allowed him to get deep inside of me as we had sex. It felt so good to me that a little tear came down my right eye. I burst into tears and cried out in passion. Andre then grabbed my hand and moved it towards his face so I could see that he was also crying. We connected sexually, but we were not in love with each other. Instead of demanding respect, I took what the men in my life were willing to give me. I didn't know how to honor myself or demand more from the men I gave myself to. Because I felt empty, I needed someone to fill me up even if that person was just as misguided and broken as I was.

A couple months later, I was pregnant. I had birth control pills but hadn't been taking them regularly as I was supposed to do. Once again, I was pregnant by a guy I didn't want to be with forever. I especially didn't want a baby with a guy who had already made another girl pregnant. I didn't even give Andre a vote. I told him that he needed to get half the money so that I could have an abortion. He was ashamed that he had gotten two girls pregnant within months of each other. Andre got his half of the money.

I was not thinking about the life of the baby. My only focus was to get rid of the problem as quickly as possible. I didn't tell my mother directly about the abortion plan. Instead, I left the yellow pages open on the kitchen table to the abortion clinics. I guess I was hoping she would see it and intervene against my plan, but she didn't. If she did see the abortion listings, she never mentioned it to me.

Andre and I went to a clinic on the far north side of Chicago to avoid being seen by anyone we knew. A strange thing happened during the abortion; I felt a tear rolled down my right eye, just like the one the night Andre and I had pillow sex.

The store we worked at merged with another KFC about a mile away, and I was transferred to the Madison store, where my cousin Nickey was. Andre stayed at the KFC on Chicago Avenue because it was close enough for him to walk to work. I was happy about the distance. After the abortion, I felt differently towards him. We rarely had sex because I feared I might get pregnant again. To this day, I think about the baby and how our lives might have been different.

Chapter

5

CHANGES

WHEN AJ WAS ALMOST THREE YEARS OLD, I moved from Anton's mother's house into my own place. Since I did not have a car, my day consisted of waking up around six-thirty a.m., getting AJ up and ready for preschool, and being at the bus stop by seven-twenty. After I dropped him off at school, I would catch the green line train to my new hotel job downtown.

AJ's preschool was half a day—my mom picked him up at the end of his four-hour school day.

This was AJ's and my weekday routine. Before going to work, I took him to school, after school he spent the remainder of the afternoon with my mom. I'd pick him up after work, then we'd make our way home to our apartment. Because my mom was so helpful to me, I never had to worry about having to find a babysitter. My mother and Larry enjoyed whenever I brought AJ over to visit. Although Larry and I rarely got along when I was a child, he and AJ got along very well. Larry would proudly introduce AJ as his grandson.

On the nights I did not feel like cooking, we would stop by the Church's Chicken restaurant that was near our apartment to pick up dinner. I parented AJ the way I thought a good mother should. I made sure we were home and in bed by nine p.m. I read to him before his bedtime and would have him read to me as he got older. I did my best to instill in him the importance of taking up for himself if someone tried to bully him. I avoided having him around people I knew were on drugs or drank alcohol excessively. I kept him close to me to ensure he also felt safe.

To establish a stable future for myself, I enrolled in a nursing medical assistant (MA) program. I wanted a career where I could help others. By choosing a new career in the healthcare field, I would have that chance. I learned to take patients' vital signs and trained as a phlebotomist. While I was in the program, my sister Chandra died.

Chandra was a college senior in Mississippi at the time of her death. Upon hearing of her death, I fell backwards against the wall. My mother was in the kitchen of her apartment crying, yelling "not my daughter." Once she saw me, she looked me in my eyes and said, "your sister is gone."

As children, Chandra and I would play house. As the oldest, she was always the mother, and I had to be the child that she told what to do. She made fun of me because I wasn't as smart as she was. To get her back, I'd fight with her and pull her hair. She'd get upset and stop taunting me. She was my big sister, so I'd still follow her around even when she was mad at me.

Later as preteens, we had separate sets of friends. Chandra and her friends were the smart ones, mines were the mischievous ones. We'd play jump rope in the open area of the project while families were going to-and-fro instead of going to the playground area. On hot summer days we would make water balloons and throw them at other children as they exited the elevator.

What I remember about my sister is that she had a beautiful smile and would light up every room she was in—you knew when Chandra was in the room. More than being energetic, she was my big sister, and I felt protected whenever she was around.

Unlike me, Chandra didn't get emotional about much. She also didn't hold her tongue—you would know what she thought of you. As tough as she was, she had moments when she would allow me to lie underneath her as if she was my security blanket. When we wanted to get away from the other children, we would sneak away and hide in our mother's bedroom closet.

Years later, after I returned to Chicago from living in Mississippi, our bond as sisters was broken. We never talked on the phone or wrote letters through the years we were separated.

And by the time I had my son, my priorities were different—AJ was my focus.

Chandra was found dead, lying on a couch after attending a party at that same home the night before. There were several rumors swirling about the cause of her death: suicide (due to her being pregnant), accidentally taking pain medication, an unknown heart disease, or being poisoned by the ex-girlfriend of her boyfriend.

The poisoning rumor continued swelling when the ex-girlfriend left Cruger shortly after Chandra's death.

I was relieved to learn that the autopsy noted that Chandra was not pregnant. However, even though her death was ruled an accidental medication overdose, rumors remained in Cruger that she was poisoned. We may never know the truth. The police ruled that no evidence led them to suspect homicide. And the person suspected of poising her has also died.

A dear childhood friend of my mother had arranged to drive us all back to Mississippi in her family's van—Larry stayed behind. My auntie Minnie Lee met us in Cruger.

Chandra's death was a shock to our entire family. Arriving at her funeral, I remember looking up at the sky, wondering how the world was still spinning when my sister was dead. The death of my sister continues to be a mystery to me. How could such a smart young woman accidentally overdose on medication? Regardless of the true reason for her death, I am grateful that she did not want to harm herself intentionally.

By her death and choices made for us as children, I felt cheated, and this was something I have never been able to get over. Even though we were not close when she died, I always hoped that she would return to Chicago to help me to raise AJ. Nonetheless, she was happy in Cruger according to our auntie Elizabeth. I believe that to be true, especially because she was about to graduate from college with a degree in criminal justice. I loved my sister, and I miss her desperately. In remembrance of her and in an effort to carry her with me every day, her name is tattooed above my left ankle.

I learned years later that my mom was at such a loss when we had to leave Cruger without my sister. I am certain she was burden with regret for ever sending Chandra to Mississippi—how could she not feel burdened, for her daughter was dead. She shared on the ride home that she wanted to jump into the Mississippi River. The only thing that stopped her was that she didn't want to leave her grandson. My auntie Minnie Lee lost over thirty pounds after Chandra's death. My sister's death left our family missing a piece that will never be replaced.

Chapter 6

MY STRUGGLES

MY HEART WAS BROKEN FROM THE DEVAStating loss of my sister. During this time, I felt lost. I returned to the medical assistant program only to quit a few months later. I was not able to focus in the classroom, and I no longer wanted to become a medical assistant.

Instead I became a room attendant at the Tremont Hotel in downtown Chicago. Despite having to clean toilets and make beds all day, I enjoyed the job. As a housekeeper, I learned to clean, organize, and decorate. I had the opportunity to meet people from different parts of the world, including celebrities such as drag queen RuPaul, Mike Ditka (the former head coach of the Chicago Bears), and actress Valerie Harper.

There were many thoughtful guests who would leave a tip on the bed or in the bathroom for me as a thank you for cleaning their room. I would be assigned to a floor with another housekeeper. We were able to chat as we cleaned our rooms together. I liked working there because the small size of the hotel allowed the housekeepers and the front desk staff to work so closely together that we were like a family. We would eat lunch together, and on Fridays we'd meet each other after work for drinks at one of the bars in the area.

As a young mother, my priorities shifted. I grew apart from my childhood friendships with Corinn and Crystal. I mainly hung around with Nickey because she was just as square as I was. When I wanted to go out to a bar or club, I'd go with my friends from the Tremont.

I stopped hanging around the old neighborhood because the drug epidemic in the nineties had taken over the community, and some of the most beautiful girls and women, after getting hooked on crack, turned into tricks. They would perform sexual favors for drugs. Many of the acts took place in an abandoned building or in an alley adjacent to my mom's basement apartment. Anyone could walk in on them, even children. The guys in my neighborhood who sold drugs either went to jail or were murdered. A week did not go by without hearing that someone had gotten arrested or killed. I disassociated myself, because I didn't even want to be tempted to do drugs, especially not crack cocaine, which was the drug of choice for many others at that time.

To keep AJ occupied while I worked, I enrolled him into a pre-kindergarten program that was within walking distance from my mother's house. On the first day of the program, while finalizing some paperwork with the director, I told her my son's name is Anton Strong Jr. but that we called him AJ. She informed me that he would be called Anton while in their program. I didn't have any kind of emotional reaction to her firm words. However, she had for sure checked me. With that, I had no doubt that AJ would be in good hands with a woman like her at the helm. She was a strong, educated black woman and unapologetic about what she knew, who she was, and what she would not tolerate from the children or their parents.

The money I earned working at the Tremont allowed me to move into a better apartment for AJ and me. AJ's pre-kindergarten program was only a half-day. I would call my mom on my lunch break to make sure that she had picked him up. I let her know when I would be getting off work to pick him up from her house. AJ and I would usually make it home by six p.m. When I had to work on a weekend, AJ stayed with his paternal grandmother. My mom still drank every weekend, but Anton's mother did not drink alcohol or smoke cigarettes. She worked at one of the local colleges during the week and on weekends enjoyed time with her grandson.

As AJ was developing from a baby to a little boy, my brother, Terry, was careening into his reckless years. He was sixteen when someone spotted him selling drugs in our neighborhood and told our mom. He'd been barking "Rocks! Blow!" to the cars driving by. My mom was terrified that Terry could get arrested or killed and sent him to live with auntie Minnie Lee in Milwaukee.

I thought of my mother as a woman overwhelmed by the responsibility of her own children. I had built up so much resentment against my mom from my childhood abuse and neglect, especially for the separation between Chandra and me. By the time she sent Terry to live in Milwaukee, I firmly believed that she never fought for us. My mother did not know how to care for us. She allowed life to happen to her instead of making thoughtful life choices for us. In addition to the choices she did and didn't make for us, we were also at the mercy of the times when she avoided decisions, like when she sent her children to someone else to raise during tough times.

The final straw for her and Larry came after twenty years of cheating and abuse. During a visit to Milwaukee, a neighbor told my mom that Larry had women coming to their apartment the entire week she was away. My family in Milwaukee had been trying for years to get my mom and me to move to Milwaukee. Surprisingly, she instructed me to have my cousins Chris and Johnnie rent a truck to get her. They arrived with a large U-Haul the same weekend to make sure she didn't change her mind.

They were disappointed that I was not going to move to Milwaukee with my mom. I told them that I was never going to leave Chicago. Admittedly, I felt conflicted when she moved to Milwaukee. In my eyes, her only saving grace was how much she loved AJ and was willing to babysit him without charging me. As a single mother, I relied on her to help me to care for AJ while I worked.

Once my mom had moved away, I was able to lean on Anton's mother and my auntie Erma, Nickey's mom, to help me with AJ, who was five at that time. Auntie Erma took care of AJ, Nickey's daughter Angel, and four adopted children between ages eight to eleven. I'd earned a promotion at work from room attendant to front desk operator. The change was welcome, but it caused me to work first and second shifts. Because AJ's grandmother was part of our care network and available any weekend, I was able to arrange my schedule to work mornings during the week and evenings on weekends. Most of my coworkers were in their twenties and enjoyed having their weekends off, so I always had takers to swap schedules.

Anton had moved from Chicago to Rockford, Illinois, where he lived with his new girlfriend. When he moved forty-five minutes away, he gave me even more reason to resent him. He was no longer able to help me with the day-to-day tasks in raising our son. He never called or sent any money. At that point, I decided I didn't need him. I never said anything negative to AJ about his dad—I decided I would allow him to make up his own mind as he got older. AJ never asked for his dad. Anton's brothers would help by taking AJ to the barber shop or to see a movie. Anton's excuse for not coming around was that the drive from Rockford was too long and he worked the evening shifts.

Anytime I talked with Anton, he had a chip on his shoulders. I'm sure he resented me because of how we broke up. I did not care, because I resented him as well for ruining my senior year of high school by getting me pregnant. Yep, I blamed him for it all. It took several years to acknowledge my part in ruining my own senior year.

Despite having us as his parents AJ was the sweetest, most well-mannered child I knew. I adored him, and he loved me. For that reason, I desperately desired to meet a man that could be a positive role model for my son.

Chapter

7

SEEKING A MAN

AT THIS POINT, AJ WAS SIX YEARS OLD AND ABLE to attend school full time. I had been single for a couple of years, and I started to miss the sound of a man's voice in my ear. I continued to do well at the hotel where I was promoted to a reservations' agent. This role allowed me to work closely with the sales team, where I got to have dinners and free drinks on the company's dime.

All was well, except I could not find a boyfriend I wanted and who wanted me.

I was in my twenties, and I had many short-lived relationships. My failure in relationships continued to happen as I kept trying to create a picture of what I wanted my life to be. I continued to pick men who were ill-equipped to live up to the mental picture I had of what my partner should be. I had yet to understand that you draw to you a reflection of who you are within yourself. Therefore, I went around in circles for years.

There was Jerry the Muslim, who was the best friend of Nickey's boyfriend Frank. Jerry acted as if he was in love with me after one date. There was also Tim, Frank's neighbor, who was obsessed with the O. J. Simpson trial—once the trial ended, so did the relationship. Al the cook and wannabe rapper broke up with me with a note. Eric was the sweetheart athlete who never got upset with me even after I destroyed his high school jersey—I broke up with him because he was too nice. Lastly, there was Mr. Unattractive who I left naked and tied to his bed with tube socks and handcuffs after he cheated on me.

I did not understand at the time that I was choosing these men because I could not identify the broken areas in my life. I was trying to fix everything I thought was wrong with me with a relationship. None of it worked; I had no control over anyone else's action, just my own.

I've never been addicted to a substance, but I can't look back on my life and not reflect on the hunger for attention and affection I desired to have from a man in my life. It came from not knowing my biological dad. I longed for a relationship with my father, even just to be able to say "my father said…" Moreover, I envied any girls, especially little girls, that had a special bond with their dads.

To deal with my "daddy's issues," I needed a man to love me, want me, and fill the void not having a father left in my soul. During a two-to-three-year span, I tagged along with Larry's niece Shakey. We joined her mom and her mom's friends at a local bar, where we flirted with men. As a joke for the men buying us drinks, we would pay them with fake dollars called "vagina coupons." It was all in jest; however, a couple of the guys tracked down Shakey and me to see if we would go out with them. Of course, we turned them down.

I handled men based upon what I wanted from them in the moment. If I was feeling lonely, I'd call up an old boyfriend to ask if I could come over. He'd say yes, we'd have sex, then I would leave. Even though I desired to be in a committed relationship, even to get married, nonetheless I found it difficult to trust men.

I finally got to the point where I was tired of having empty sex and I thought I should create a spiritual foundation for my son and me.

Neither my mom nor any of the other adults in our home ever took us to church; however, she and my auntie Minnie Lee would always encourage us to pray to God whenever we needed help. In addition, a hair stylist I went to would often talk about how blessed she was and how she enjoyed going to church. She was very beautiful and successful. I wanted a piece of the happiness she was experiencing.

Frank's mom was the only other woman I knew who went to church on a regular basis. She would pick up AJ and me each Sunday morning, and we would go to church with her. The experience was odd, because we sat way up on the top level of the church. I could not understand anything the preacher was talking about. AJ and I went for a few weeks, then we stopped going altogether. Still wanting to raise AJ up to know God, I started to go with him to a smaller church that was around the corner from our apartment building. We had been going there for a few weeks when I decided that AJ and I would get baptized. The church was so small we had to go to one of their sister churches for the baptism. After the baptism, a lady and her sister were kind enough to drive AJ and me back home. While we were in the car, one of the ladies asked me if I felt any different after being baptized. I did not want to disappoint her, so I said, yes, I felt different. The lady and her sister both shouted, "Praise the Lord!" then they continued to drive us home.

The truth was that I did not feel any different after the baptism. I continued to go to the church for a few more months, then I quit going there as well. I was tired of being a single mother. I needed help with raising my son. I could not find the answer in the church. I decided that I would fix my life on my own. That decision led me to think that I should get back together with Anton. I thought that no one would be better to help me raise AJ than his father.

I called Anton and shared my thoughts with him. I told him how exhausted I was feeling. Continuing, I mentioned that if he was willing to forgive me for my part in our relationship ending, I was open to getting back together so we could raise our son together. Anton's girlfriend was not a factor in my decision. Even though I had broken up with him, I had no doubt that he would leave his girlfriend for me. I had his heart. I left it up to him to decide how to break up with her.

Later that week, Anton drove to Chicago so we could talk some more. He sat in the chair, while I sat on the couch directly across from him. Anton was arrogant; he often acted like nothing bothered him, even when it did. He would allow things to pile up, then he would explode. For that reason, I allowed him to do most of the talking that night. He let me know how badly I had hurt him. He shared how he could not go through that again. I let him know that I had no intention of hurting him again and that I needed his help. He mentioned how his mom was willing to help me out anytime I needed her to. I reminded him that his mother was not AJ's father. We went back and forth weighing our options, then I told him to just think about moving in with AJ and me.

I asked him to let me know his decision the following week. The evening had gotten late. I told Anton he could spend the night with me if he did not want to drive back to Rockford. He decided to stay the night at his mother's house instead. As he got up to leave, he kissed me (or I kissed him), then we started to make our way to my bedroom.

Once we made it to the bed, Anton became hesitant. I thought he did not want to have sex with me. He said it wasn't that. He was just nervous about us being together again; he couldn't believe it. I laid him on his back and got on top of him. We both knew we were making a huge mistake. Despite our apprehension, Anton moved in the following week.

Chapter 8

RECONNECTION

AFTER ANTON MOVED IN, IT TOOK NO TIME FOR me to regret the decision for us to live together. Anton had been living in my apartment with AJ and me for a few months. Despite my desires for us to create an environment for our son that would have his father and mother under one roof, it felt artificial.

To be fair, I expected much from Anton that he was incapable of giving me. I wanted our story to be one where despite the odds, we pulled together to create a loving home environment for our son. The truth was we no longer liked one another as individuals. He despised me for wanting him to be a man that measured up to my idea of what a successful man looked like. And I resented him for not having any drive to move beyond our neighborhood.

I was trying my best to give our son what I missed out on as a child. Of course, it did not work. I could not fix my childhood trauma by having my son in a two-parent home. Moreover, I never made my expectations clear to Anton. The initial invitation was for us to make things easier for childcare, not a relationship for him and me per se. I'd hoped he'd eventually get it and play his role as the happy father—he never did. Instead Anton and I were more like roommates than a young couple raising our son.

Like roommates, we split the bills between the two of us. We only saw each other in passing. I worked a regular shift from nine a.m. to five p.m. at the hotel; Anton worked a second shift from three p.m. to eleven p.m. as a custodian at a factory. The differences in our work schedules worked out fine for us to ensure that AJ was taken to school and childcare. I drove Anton's car to and from work whenever he had a day off during the week.

Unlike our son's schedule, our relationship was on shaky ground. We both cared greatly for our son; therefore, we suffered through living together, especially me. Anton was often moody. In spite of that, I was determined to create a caring homelife. I made dinner each night for the three of us, and we had sex on most nights, even though I was tired by the time he made it home from work. I foolishly thought if I'd treated him like my husband, he would become my husband.

Whenever Anton was not asleep, he was either melancholy or joyful. He was very secretive about where he spent his time.

He would often say that he was at his mother's house. However, whenever I talked with her, she would unknowingly mention that she had not seen him. This typically happened every other weekend—coinciding with his payday from work.

I began to gain weight, and my spirit started feeling dark. I started drinking more and more on the weekends to dull my frustration, loneliness, and sadness. On the weekdays, I would put on a happy face and pretend that everything was fine, but I was miserable. My plan to build a happy home was failing terribly. I became numb and too embarrassed to share my pain with anyone, even Nickey. I thought life was better for everyone else. So I avoided seeing my family and friends around this time and focused on my work at the hotel.

Anton was young and handsome, with a beautiful body, and every night he wanted to have sex. I did not always enjoy having sex with him. It often felt like checking something off my to-do list rather than having a connection with my partner. It was as if he was trying to make up for lost time when we were not together. For me, sex with him was something I did to minimize the arguments.

We constantly argued about him wanting to have sex all the time. We also argued about his lack of ambition. I wanted more out of life and was willing to work hard to get. He was content with the crumbs.

It didn't help that when I wouldn't have sex with him, he'd accuse me of cheating on him. Seeing how our relationship had fallen made me heartbreakingly sad. When we first started seeing each other, I would get such a big smile on my face whenever Anton walked into a room. Now we avoided being in the same room together whenever possible.

Anton had been the victim of a racially motivated prank at his job, and we agreed that he should leave. I didn't expect him to quit the same day, without finding a new job. I suppose that's the nature of a protest, but we weren't prepared for living on just one income. The financial strain made us argue even more.

I started to get more promotions at work and invitations to attend special events and company parties. The other invited guests didn't grow up in the "hood," like Anton and me. This exposure to other upbringings and other ways of living and seeing the world helped me envision a life with more than just weekend drinking.

Anton came to one party and felt uncomfortable the entire time. He never accompanied me again. He shared with me that he thought I was too good for him and would leave him at any moment.

He had gone through my address book, leaving it on our kitchen table for me to find. He'd included a note chastising me for keeping a book with so many men's names and phone numbers. The notebook listed mostly family, both men and women, and close friends. His note accused me of planning to see one of them again one day. To appease him, I crossed out the names of men who were not members of my family. I crossed out my own name, too, and left the notebook on the table for him to see.

I didn't know that Anton's behavior was a form of abuse. I thought abuse was only things such as punching and hitting. Anton had been controlling ever since we learned about AJ. Once I became pregnant, Anton felt as if he owned me and that he could tell me what to do because I was carrying his baby. Back then I allowed him to think that was true because I felt stuck. From the beginning I wanted my children to have the same father—I judged my mother, because my siblings and I all had different fathers. And the last thing I wanted was to be anything like my mother. As fate would have it, "For the thing which I greatly feared is come upon me, and that which I was afraid of is come unto me" (Job 3:25 KJV).

Despite knowing I would want more children, I knew I did not want more children with Anton.

Now that we were living together, I could see the behavior for the possessiveness it was. He was trying to find ways to ding my pride as I became confident in my work. When I earned a second promotion in less than a year, he suggested that I was in an inappropriate relationship with my boss, as if I couldn't have gotten those promotions on my own merit.

It all came to a head when we made plans to visit my family for the upcoming Thanksgiving holiday. Days before the holiday visit, I found a mini plastic bag in Anton's car with crack cocaine. I was angry, not just because I was potentially living with a person on drugs, but that he was also careless; our son could have found the bag instead of me. I knew we'd need to address the drugs soon, but I decided not to mention my discovery before our holiday vacation to Milwaukee.

Friday night after Thanksgiving, I was at auntie Minnie Lee and uncle Pookey's house visiting and Anton went out drinking with my cousin Johnnie and some of his friends. I'd packed up for our drive back to Chicago the next day and fallen asleep after I'd put AJ to bed. My cousin's girlfriend shook me awake to tell me that Anton was drunk, had my keys, and was trying to drive back to Chicago. I jumped out of the bed and ran out of the house to see Anton as he was getting into the driver's seat.

I confronted him through the car window, and he slurred about me treating him like "a motherfucking fool" and said that I hadn't been visiting family but fooling around with another man. I climbed into the passenger side to calm him down. I lost patience quickly and told him how ridiculous he sounded. He ordered me out of the car; I refused. It was my car, I reminded him.

At that moment, he peels away from the curb, incoherently yelling what a terrible person I was. He didn't know the way to the highway exit, and we careened around corners and down residential streets. I begged him to please turn the car around. Rigid with fear, I continued to plead with him, but he would not listen to me. Suddenly, I heard a loud crash as my body jerked quickly towards the dashboard. He had run my car into a fire hydrant a few blocks away.

Neither of us were physically hurt from the impact of crash. Instantly, I was overwhelmed by the thought that Anton had intentionally crashed into the hydrant. He was unwilling to admit he didn't know his way back to Chicago, so to save face in addition to hurt me, he crashed my car. It may sound irrational; nevertheless, I believe that to be true.

Within minutes, Milwaukee police surrounded my car, yelling at us to turn off the car and get out with our hands up. Anton got out immediately, as if being pulled over by police was routine. I got out of the car slowly, still wearing my nightgown, with tears running down my face. An officer pulled me to one corner and another officer had Anton a few feet from the wreckage of the car. The fire department came along to shut off the water rushing from the fire hydrant. The officer told me to explain what had happened, and I did.

After she conferred with the other officer, she returned to me and told me that she would drive me back to my cousin's house. Anton was arrested for damaging city property. While the officer was explaining that I would need to call my insurance company to report what happened to my car, her voice appeared to come from miles away. Because it was a holiday weekend, Anton would not be able to have a bail hearing until Monday morning.

The next day, my cousin Chris drove me and AJ back home to Chicago. I called Anton's mom to let her know what had happened and that he was in jail. She asked why I had not called her when Anton first got arrested. I had no answer for her. The question left me feeling bewildered. At the time, I could not careless about Anton's arrest and sorting out his emergency contacts. My son and my car—that was it.

After speaking with Anton's mom, I packed up his belongings, put them into his car, drove it all to her house, and gave her the keys. He was released on a cash bond after a few days in jail. He came to my apartment to try to explain himself. I did not want to hear anything he had to say. He kept trying to tell me that he and I both made mistakes that night. At that point, I was so over the drama of my relationship with him that nothing he could say would cause me to take him back. At that very moment, my desire to have a complete family unit was over.

The only part that broke my heart was that I had to explain to AJ, who was about five or six years old, that his dad would no longer be living with us. AJ then asked, "So, I won't be able to see my dad anymore?" I let him know that he could see his dad whenever he wanted to do so. As I continued to console my son, I let him know that we were going to be fine. I was not sure if I was trying to convince AJ or myself.

One night, Anton came to my door drunk wanting to talk about our relationship, and I was stunned. It was as if I was living someone else's life. Anton was never a heavy drinker. I think he got drunk in order to build up his nerve to talk to me. He told me that he wanted us to have sex. I let him know that he'd better not put his hands on me. He was toxic to me now. Everything he did or said reminded me of my mother's relationship with Larry. But unlike my mother, I was not going to spend the next twenty years with someone that I knew was no good for me, nor me for him.

Nonetheless, he was my son's father, and he was drunk. I allowed him to sleep it off on my couch. While hanging up his jacket, I found in his pocket another one of those mini plastic bags containing crack cocaine. This discovery explained Anton's erratic behavior. Just before he got ready to leave the next morning, I told him that we could still be together if he took the crack and flushed it down the toilet in front of me. He looked me in my eyes and said that he couldn't do it.

Our relationship was over for real this time. I could not be with someone who used drugs. I knew I would not be able to trust them. I had witnessed too much destruction in my community and had seen how individuals on drugs would steal DVD players and televisions from their own mother's houses and sell them for ten dollars to buy crack cocaine. Now my son's father was one of them.

Anton did not want me to think that he was a crackhead who would steal things out of someone's house. Instead, he'd asked. He came to borrow my DVD player one day. He said he needed the pawn shop money but would buy back the DVD player once he got his check the next week. I allowed him to take the DVD player, but I knew I would never see it again. I just replaced it and never allowed Anton back in my apartment.

Thanksgiving had rolled back around, and AJ and I were looking forward to our annual visit to Milwaukee. When we got home and were getting ready to pack, I noticed a piece of wood was missing from the door. My heart dropped because I knew someone had broken into our apartment. As I looked around, I expected to see things thrown all around the apartment, but everything was in order. The only items taken were the DVD player, AJ's video game console, and a video recorder.

The police came right away and dusted for fingerprints. I called Anton to let him know about the break-in. Because he was AJ's father, I wanted to let him know what happened. I told him I couldn't go to Milwaukee to spend the holiday with family because of the break-in. Anton was calm and dispassionate, so I said I would talk to him later and hung up the phone.

I called my auntie Minnie Lee's house to let them know I wouldn't make the trip. My cousin Sammie answered the phone. He got really upset when I told him about the break-in. It was the reaction I expected from Anton. When I spoke with my cousin Chris, his first comment was, "Jennifer, it was Anton."

I insisted Anton wouldn't, couldn't do that to me or his son. Chris pushed back, declaring with certainty that it was Anton. I quickly got off the phone and dismissed what Chris had said. Sometime later, as I pondered the break-in further, it seemed reasonable to me that Anton might have broken into my apartment instead of a stranger, particularly because the apartment was pretty much untouched except for the stolen items. A stranger might have left things thrown around all over the place. What finally convinced me even more of Anton's guilt was his lack of anger and failure to ask what happened during the break-in.

The thought that Anton could have so much disregard for my safety or his son was the breaking point; I knew I needed to take the next step and move my family to Milwaukee. I was devastated and heartbroken that Anton's drug use could bring him to the point where he would steal from me. I never asked Anton if he was the one that broke into the apartment. Instead, I told him that I no longer felt safe in Chicago.

I told my family in Chicago and Milwaukee and a few close friends that I would be relocating once AJ's school semester was over. Nickey was more distraught than anyone about the move. At that time, she and I were more like sisters than cousins. We spent most of our free time together. In addition, we had come to rely upon one another to help raise our children.

Nickey knew that I had said repeatedly over the years that I would never move to Milwaukee. I felt differently now, because I had this instinctive feeling that I needed to leave Chicago to protect my son and me. Still, I do not think Nickey believed that I would truly leave Chicago until the moment she saw the moving truck take off.

Chapter 9

MILWAUKEE

IN THE SUMMER OF 1999, I WAS LIVING IN Milwaukee. I previously only visited this city during celebratory times—cousins' birthday parties, weddings, or holidays. Now I had to learn to see Milwaukee as my home. I had no idea what the city had to offer me—all I did know was that it was not Chicago. Fortunately, Milwaukee is only ninety miles away from downtown Chicago. Whenever I missed being in Chicago or whenever any close friends or family members had a special event, I made sure to go. I just made the quick drive down Interstate 94.

After a few months of traveling back and forth between Milwaukee and Chicago, I decided that I had to stop trying to hold onto Chicago as if it was an ex-lover I couldn't let go.

Over time, I grew to find some peace about living in Milwaukee. However, I needed to find a stable job. For the first six months while living in Milwaukee I did temp jobs, providing administrative support until I could find something permanent in the hospitality industry.

The organization that managed the Tremont in Chicago also managed a Sheraton in Brookfield. I didn't apply to any other hotel chains, but only to the Sheraton. I was already anticipating feeling the same family vibe I had enjoyed at the Tremont at the Sheraton in Brookfield.

Unfortunately, when I received the call from the human resources manager, she offered me a housekeeping job, not the administrative position I'd applied for. I was insulted. Either she hadn't read my resume or assumed that I, as a young Black woman, would be happy with whatever job she offered me. She told me I could become the housekeeping supervisor after a few months, then the manager. I graciously declined, letting her know I had no interest in housekeeping, but she could contact me if an administrative position opened in sales and catering.

Within a couple weeks, the HR manager called me once again to let me know that an administrative assistant role had opened that I could interview for. I would be working directly with Jeff, the director of catering. I let her know that I would love to interview with Jeff.

My assertiveness paid off. The following week, I met Jeff and interviewed for a position in sales and catering. During the interview, the manager kept yawning. I was giving my best and worried that either I or my stories were falling short. At one point, Jeff, apologized for his sluggishness, describing the two-wedding weekend he had managed on his own. Without missing a beat, I assured him that he wouldn't have to work so hard with me on the team. I got hired on the spot.

Once I started working at the Sheraton, my life felt normal again. I met a woman named Elnora who would become one of my dearest friends during my time at the Sheraton. She gave me the lay of the land in the sales office. As a Black woman herself, she let me know who was trustworthy and who I should stay away from. Even though Elnora was fifteen years older than me, I liked her a lot. We had sons the same age, and she reminded me of my cousin Nickey. Elnora and Nickey both had the gift of gab and looked out for me and my son.

For the time being, AJ and I lived with auntie Minnie Lee and uncle Pookey. The house was a two-story home with two bedrooms on the main level and four bedrooms on the second story. The house was so big that our entire immediate family could live under the same roof most days. Auntie Minnie Lee cooked for everyone every night. Anyone who was not living in the house would visit on the weekends.

My first cousins (Sammie, Johnnie, Chris, and Falesia) and I were in our mid to late twenties. My brother Terry and younger cousins Peaches and Pooh were teenagers now. I again never had to worry about finding a babysitter, because my mom lived in the same house as well. Sammie gave up the large second-floor bedroom so AJ and I could move in. AJ enjoyed being there because he was able to play with Falesia's children, Tristan, EJ, and Domnesha.

Though my family was close, we mainly lived our own lives during the week and would come together on most weekends to drink and talk about the good old days. I enjoyed being able to spend time with my family; however, as the weeknights drew closer to an end, I would find myself pondering if life had more than this—drinking just to get drunk.

I used the drinking to mask the feelings of loneliness I still couldn't shake. I loved my family dearly; however, I knew there was more for me than drinking every weekend. What that "more" could be I didn't know, but I had decided to go searching for it.

My first certain step was to enroll in the local two-year school. I had only completed my high school diploma and knew that anything more I had in mind for myself would require higher learning. I registered at Milwaukee Area Technical College (MATC) in the human services degree program. I learned about cultural differences, addictive behavior, and effective communication skills.

I was able to finish the program within three years, including an internship, all while caring for my son and working full-time. I also managed to get AJ and me our own place. He was ten, and it was time to move out of auntie Minnie Lee and uncle Pookey's home.

In all my new busyness—AJ, work, and school—I rarely got to see my family. I felt a loneliness closing in again. I was longing for connections with people. As the famous quote from the poet Rumi goes, "what you seek is seeking you."

First, I took AJ's suggestion and started looking for a church. The only way I remember church coming up as a child was when my mom or my auntie Minnie Lee would talk about not going to church because of how often they had to attend as kids. As recently as my last weekend in the big house drinking and playing cards, my mom and auntie laughed about going back to church once they stopped drinking.

I didn't know what to expect, but I felt my son had offered us a sound idea. I found a small church that wasn't far from my apartment. We sat in the back pews because I didn't think someone with all my mistakes could sit in the front row in church. AJ and I went to that church for almost two years, but I never joined. One afternoon, I overhead the deacon and the pastor speaking negatively about one of the members. That was my last Sunday there.

Even though that ministry wasn't healthy, I'd clearly picked up healthy new tools in God's house. Rather than fretting and complaining or confronting the pastor and deacon, I turned to God. At this point, I was lost, and I knew it. I wanted to seek wisdom in a spiritual sense, and not just in academia. I prayed to God to connect me to a church with members who truly loved Him and a pastor who could teach me how to understand the Bible for myself and didn't preach in sugar-coated sermons.

Until I could find a new physical church, I fed my spirit on Sundays by tuning in to different church broadcasts. I soon listened exclusively to Walter Harvey, the pastor of the Parklawn Assembly of God. After listening for a few months, I decided to visit. The people greeted AJ and me with friendly smiles. I chose to sit in the back of the church again. As the months went by, I was drawn closer and closer to the altar. After two years, AJ and I sat in the row right behind the pastors' and elders' seats.

In this same window of yearning and learning, I found another tribe. I started hearing radio advertisements about a weekly poetry open mic taking place at a neighborhood bar just minutes from my apartment. On Thursday nights, I made sure I was at the Mecca.

I was hooked from the first night. I asked the bartender if the poetry show would be starting soon. He called over the owner of the bar, Dasha Kelly. She was a tall, beautiful lady with natural curly hair. She had a Whitney Houston kind of vibe; she didn't present as a diva but was decidedly a cut above the rest. I let her know that it was my first time and that I was excited to hear poetry that night. Dasha gave me a smile and gave a quick rundown of the sign-up list, open seating, and special performances.

The night was incredible. I was enthralled from the moment Dasha welcomed me. And soon the audience of folks would become another family—all the way to the last poet. Every artist who performed that night was a star, and I watched them all sparkle and glow every week. One man named Malcolm immediately caught my eye. When I watched him perform, I had to remind myself to breathe.

He commanded the room when he began to speak. I could not look away; I wanted to capture each word he recited. I fell quickly and hard for Malcolm and began to think about how I could get closer to him. Of course, he had no idea that I existed, but I was determined to change that. I began showing up to all his performances around town.

One night after one of his shows, I was one of the last individuals there, hanging around and talking with the artist and other performers. As I began to gather my things to leave, Malcolm offered to walk me to my car. I quickly said yes. While we were walking, I let him know that I had written a poem for him. The poem basically declared how amazing I thought he was and how he made me want to be a better person. I asked him if he wouldn't mind giving me feedback. After handing him the poem, I told him I wasn't like every other person who tells him he's special. We both smiled. I was about to double down and tell him I was serious, but Malcolm raised his finger to my lips and told me to go home.

The next day at work, I grabbed Elnora to tell her all about my time alone with Malcolm. "He finally knows my name!" I said to her. Elnora laughed at me and called me crazy. She said, "He's just a man." She started relating a story from a "Malcolm" in her past, but I wasn't listening. Malcolm was different from any other man on the planet, particularly because he had a desire to want to help children in the Milwaukee community. I saw him as a magical neighborhood superhero.

One night, I called Malcolm and asked if he wanted to come over to watch a movie. To my surprise, he said yes; I was overjoyed. I began to sweat with excitement at the thought that I was going to have sex with my superhero! I quickly prepared AJ for his bedtime and tucked him into bed, gently closing his bedroom door behind me. I brushed my teeth and took a shower. Having Malcolm in my apartment felt as if I was entertaining a superstar—not because he saw himself that way but because of the high regard I felt for him. When he arrived, we talked more than watched the movie.

When Malcolm was not performing, he had a quiet demeanor. He often kept to himself, becoming animated when others wanted him to perform. When he was around me, he knew he didn't have to perform at all; he just needed to be himself.

Whenever I found myself home alone and Malcolm was available, we would be making out in my bedroom and comforting each other about things going on in our lives. When together, we shared some of our most intimate and private thoughts. As far as I was aware, no one in our poetry family knew we were as close as we were; we were fine with that.

Every time I thought of him, I got butterflies, and every time he touched me, I became breathless. Elnora thought it was weird that we only hung out in my room making out and watching movies. For me, our connection was not just infatuation. He got me to think differently about the suffering in our community. She told me he must be hiding something and that I deserved to be with someone open and available to love me publicly.

I knew what Elnora was telling me was correct, but I was hooked. Malcolm and I would fool around up to the point of having sex, without actual intercourse. Malcolm was a Muslim. With that, we ultimately knew that we could never be together because of our different faiths. Malcolm would tell me that we couldn't have sex because I didn't belong to him. I assumed that he felt that way because we were not married to each other.

Sometime later, I got a call from a mutual friend in the poetry community. She told me to guess who was getting married and blurted out Malcolm's name before I could answer. Obviously, I was shocked by the news, though my reasons were different from our friend's. Malcolm was someone many women wanted, but he kept most of them at arms' length. I had mistakenly imagined that he thought differently about me.

My shock hardened to fury. Malcolm didn't answer when I called, so I left a voice message saying that he could have given me a heads-up that he was getting married. It was obvious to me that what we shared was meaningless to him since he allowed me to hear about him getting married on the streets. After leaving the voicemail, Malcolm and I did not speak until a few years later, after he was divorced.

The initial news that Malcolm was getting married left me in such a state of shock and devastation that I started seeking help from God.

Going to church, even twice a week, was not enough. I needed reinforcement, so I began listening to other pastors whose sermons were broadcast daily like, Bishop T. D. Jakes, Joel Osteen, Joseph Prince, and Joyce Meyer. In addition, I read a Bible verse each day and tried to see how it applied to my life.

I began to see more clearly that trying to get a man or keep a man was not the issue. I needed to learn what God had to say about me. Listening to Bishop Jakes, Joyce Meyer, and others got me to see that my choices brought me to where I was then—I could no longer blame others, for the enemy was in me. According to Joyce, I needed to "think about what I was thinking about."

Pastor Joel Osteen helped me to see that God had a plan for my life that would go beyond my wildest dreams. Pastor Joseph Prince helped me to see that the grace of God could heal me from any addiction. I just needed to know that just as Jesus is in heaven, so am I on the earth—Jesus is healthy and whole in heaven, and so am I on the earth.

The verse of the day I received included a message about daily living. These additional steps got me to see how harmful it was to gossip about others and the importance of praying instead of complaining.

As I prayed regularly and studied the Bible, my confidence began to increase. I was able to appreciate the people in my life instead of being critical of them.

I'd fallen in love with Jesus, and because of His love for me, I was able to say yes to God's will for my life.

Chapter
10

Helplessness

BY THE TIME I WAS READY TO SAY YES TO GOD, I had hit the proverbial rock bottom. Emotionally and energetically, I felt as though I could not catch a break. I wallowed in a constant state of sadness, loneliness, and brokenness. Even though my life appeared to be going well—my son was happy and healthy, and I had a great job, good friends, and my own apartment—I still found myself wanting a man to share my life with. However, either I was not attracted to the men who would approach me, or the ones I was attracted to would already be in a relationship with someone else.

I began to learn that I was drawing those type of men to me because I had not dealt with the brokenness in my life. Until I became a healthier woman, there was no way I was going to draw a healthy man to me.

The truth is I was not capable then of trusting anyone. I felt that if I would ever be open and honest and share my truth, especially with a man, he would judge me or not give me the same honesty in return.

Of course, others around me had no idea of the internal struggles I was dealing with. I never trusted anyone enough to share my whole true self with them. Trauma kept me from allowing people to get too close to me. I carried dreadful thoughts that people would die, desert me, or not measure up to some arbitrary standard I placed on them.

When I said yes to God, I had no idea what I was saying yes to. I was not sure what having a relationship with God really meant or just how broken I truly was. All I knew was that I had gotten it all wrong for so long and that I had hit rock bottom again. At that point, the only place for me to go from there was up. For me, it was going to take more than just going to Parklawn Assembly of God church every week and listening to television Pastors. I also attended Parklawn's Wednesday night Bible study. In addition, each Monday night I participated in a weekly cell group meeting led by Edna Mathews in her home.

Edna is one of those spiritual mothers who will not allow you to feel sorry for yourself. She would constantly say to me, "Well, what does the Bible say about that thing?" Regardless of what the situation was, she would remind me to compare it to the Word of God. The cell group meetings (Bible study sessions) were attended by up to fifteen different Christian women, many of whom I still share a close relationship with today.

The Bible study sessions would last for a couple of hours each week. At the meeting, we dissected the previous Sunday's sermon by Pastor Harvey and discussed how it was applicable to our lives. By this time, AJ was a teenager and had begun getting into trouble at school. He was smoking marijuana and sneaking out of the house when he thought I had fallen asleep. I was clueless as to how to discipline a teenage boy. My solution was to take away the things that he liked most and make him write in a journal about his behavior in school. He was also supposed to show how he would make better choices. I realize now that what he really needed was me and a positive male role model. Unfortunately, I did not have the wherewithal to help my son, because I was broken. And my history of being molested did not allow me to trust men to do right by my son.

AJ and I would often have conversations about his life choices. I would remind him that if he desired to have a better life, he needed to make better life choices. He would listen to me at that moment; however, not long after our conversations ended, he would jump right back into his old habits. Ultimately, I would receive a call from the school that he was a truant or from a Milwaukee police officer that he had been picked up for getting into trouble with his cousins. When he was around sixteen years old, AJ and two of his cousins were accused of breaking into the house of one of their girlfriends, stealing some of the valuables. None of this made any sense to me. I raised AJ to respect other people, and especially himself. I knew he smoked marijuana and skipped school, but I never thought he would break into someone's house, regardless of what his cousins were doing.

This change in his behavior began to make me feel as though everything I had sacrificed for him to have a better life than mine was for nothing. He was choosing the street life over the Christian life that I wanted for him.

He began to reject church and God and decided he no longer wanted to go to church with me. I took it as a personal rejection of me as well.

Instead of trying to figure things out on my own, this time, I turned to God and my Christian sisters for encouragement, prayers, and support.

Each week at the end of Edna's cell meetings, she asked if there were any prayer requests. And each week I would cry about AJ and ask the sister to pray for him and for my family. One night, while one of the other ladies in the group was praying, tears began to roll down my face. At this point, I had been attending the weekly cell meetings for a few years, and Edna must have begun to lose her patience with my constant crying about AJ.

She gave me a look that said either you are going to believe God, or you are not. So instead of allowing herself or anyone else in the group to comfort me as they normally would, Edna looked me square in my eyes and said, "Jennifer, this is the last time you are going to cry about that boy." When she said those words, a peace came over me, and my tears dried up instantly.

I believed what she said. Therefore once I got home that night, I prayed to God and said that I was getting out of His way when it came to Him raising my son. I was giving AJ back to God to allow God's will to be done in AJ's life.

Feeling peace after I prayed, I went to bed. During the night, I had a dream that God was speaking clearly to me. He said, "Do not send your son back to Chicago." God must have known that I was contemplating sending AJ back to Chicago to live with his father. Anton had been communicating with AJ, and I might have thought for two seconds of sending AJ to Anton to take care of him during his teenage years.

Once I released AJ back to God, things got even worse instead of better. The following year AJ stopped at the corner gas station. While inside, he got an overwhelming feeling that the other guys in the store were going to try to rob him. At that point, he left the store and began to walk quickly towards the bus stop. While walking, he noticed the guys were behind him, so he began to run. As he ran, one of the guys pulled a gun and began shooting at him. The last shot hit AJ in his right leg, and he fell to the ground. After he fell to the ground, the guys then jumped into their car and drove off.

While all this was going on, I was home doing laundry in the house I purchased for us just a few years earlier. It was Christmas Eve. I felt what could only be the voice of God whispering to me in my ear, "Pray for your son." Because that experience had never happened to me before, I began to pray right away for God's protection to be over AJ. Within seconds, I received a phone call from AJ's cell phone. I did not recognize the voice of the person on the other end, who told me that my son had been shot and was in the middle of the street on Sherman and Burleigh.

I thanked the person on the phone, then I yelled to my brother Terry, who was living with me. I let him know that I needed him to ride with me because someone had just shot AJ.

As we approached the scene where AJ had been shot, the police and the emergency medical technicians (EMTs) were already there and had placed AJ into the ambulance. The area where AJ had been lying was roped off. As I got closer to the scene, a police officer walked towards me, and without waiting to hear anything the officer was going to say, I said, "That is my son." He said to me, "Ma'am he is breathing and awake. The ambulance has him secured, and they are taking him to Children's Hospital." He let me know that I could meet them there.

I made it to the hospital, where a detective was waiting to ask me some questions. He wanted to know if AJ had access to a gun and if I knew of anyone who would want to hurt him. The detective seemed more interested in trying to portray AJ as a criminal than looking for the person who shot him. Shortly after speaking with the detective, I got to see AJ. He was sitting up in the hospital bed with his wounded leg wrapped up and was somewhat in a state of shock. He could not believe that this had happened to him. All he could say to me was, "Somebody shot me momma; why would anyone want to shoot me?" I had no words to help him understand what had just happened to him. All I could say was that he was going to be fine and that I was going to help him to get better.

AJ had surgery to repair the damage the bullet did to his leg, followed by six months of physical therapy to teach him how to walk again. He suffered some post-traumatic stress disorder after being shot. He did not want to go outside for a while. I found myself unable to say the words "My son was shot"; instead I referred to the situation as "the accident." My son could have died that night and saying the words "my son was shot" made it too real. It let me know that I was in control of nothing.

To help with our trauma, both AJ and I participated in the Project Ujima program, which supports victims and families who have experienced violence. The leaders of the program helped us to talk about our feelings, and they taught AJ tools to help minimize his anxiety about going outside.

Unlike my other traumatic experiences, this time I did not blame God for what happened. I was appreciative of Him and the love He showed to me and my son. I was overwhelmed that God had saved my son. By being obedient to that still small voice, I was able to pray for my son—and have a hand in stopping the evil that was trying to take his life.

The police never found the boys who shot AJ. In my opinion, they never even tried to find the shooter. To them, AJ was just another black boy on the streets of Milwaukee from the hood who got shot. They probably saw him as one of the lucky ones, because he did not die.

Doctors can patch up physical wounds, but the emotional and psychological wounds remain long after the bandages come off. I continued to pray for my son every time he walked out of my front door, and I thanked God every time he returned home.

The horror of what happened to AJ allowed me to learn that tragedies will come; nevertheless, I prefer to get through them with God rather than without Him. I choose to believe the Bible not because of what someone else told me; instead, I believe God because I experienced him for myself. I read the Bible for myself. I studied the Word of God for myself. It is not about religion for me. I have the distinct privilege of having a relationship with God.

Chapter
11

THE PARTY

I WISH I COULD SAY THAT ONCE I BEGAN TO build a personal relationship with God that my problems were all over, but that is not the truth—not in the least. I continued going to church regularly. However, I still enjoyed drinking and partying with my family and friends. I received a call from my cousin Nickey about her birthday party. I was super excited for Nickey's party! Although Milwaukee was starting to grow on me, Chicago was still my home, and no other city could take the place of my hometown. Anytime someone asks me where I'm from, I proudly say that I live in Milwaukee, but I am from Chicago.

Many may wonder why I would be so proud to come from a city with one of the highest murder rates in the country. Well, if you ask anyone my age and community why we are proud to be from Chicago we would all say because we survived when so many of our friends did not.

I owe my resiliency, my ability to overcome challenges, and my compassion towards others to the community of folks I met in the projects. Living in the projects was not chaotic all the time. Before it became overrun with drugs and gangs, it was a great community of people who supported one another and looked out for each other and their families. Some of my best life lessons were learned while growing up in the Henry Horner projects in Chicago.

We celebrate our own survival, and we celebrate those who did not survive. Their lives matter because they had an impact in our lives.

Terry rode along with me to go to Nickey's party. I booked a twin bedroom using my Sheraton Hotel employee discount for us to stay at the new W hotel in downtown Chicago. My intention was to stay at the W hotel so we could get up early the next morning and drive back to Milwaukee.

On the day of Nickey's party, Terry and I arrived in town early that afternoon. We visited our old neighborhood and hung out for a little with some of our friends and family that still lived there. We visited Larry, his sister Dallas, and her children, who were all adults now, and we could laugh about the relationship between him and our mother. Although they had broken up years earlier, we all still considered one another family.

Once we left Dallas's house, we went around the corner to go see Terry's friend Marcus. A couple of Terry's friends, including Marcus, had a crush on me since the summer they saw me sitting outside our basement apartment in my nightgown. The wind had blown the gown up a little to reveal my legs. I thought it was cute but never took them seriously. They were just Terry's dirty little friends.

"Little" Marcus was now standing in front of me with all of his muscles, handsomeness, and twenty-three years of "grown enough." When we told him about Nickey's party, he smiled at me and asked if he could go. I said sure, gave him the location, and warned him that he couldn't wear sneakers.

All the while I was getting dressed for the party, I kept replaying in my head my earlier conversation with Marcus. I kept trying to convince myself that he was not trying to flirt with me. Even if he was, there was no way I could go there for several reasons. For one, he was my brother's best friend, and I was also eight years older than him. Any thought of a relationship between Marcus and me would be wrong on so many levels. I repeated to myself that nothing was going to happen.

When we arrived at the party, there were many beautiful girls there, but Marcus kept his eyes on me the entire night. I kept trying to convince him to hang out with girls his own age. He ignored what I had to say and asked me to dance with him. After a couple of drinks, I could not ignore how much he wanted me to dance with him. As we danced, Marcus held me close to him. I told myself this was only for one night and tomorrow things would go back to normal.

For the remainder of the night Marcus and I danced and held hands. After dancing, we sat at a table, all the while continuing to hold one another's hands. Our knees came together as closely as possible. While talking to other people at our table, we continued to embrace. The connection we had that night was obvious. One of my cousins asked if we were in love; we both just laughed and continued embracing one another.

As the night was coming close to an end, I tried to give Marcus an out by telling him and Terry to take some of their girlfriends to the hotel room and that I would stay at Nickey and Frank's house for the night. Marcus insisted that he only wanted to be with me, so the three of us went to the W hotel together. Once Marcus and I thought Terry was completely drunk and in a deep sleep, we started kissing and feeling each other all over. Marcus's body felt like a black god's. His stomach had so many muscles. Instead of a six pack, he had an eight pack. All I kept thinking was, "Oh my God," as I continued touching him. As we began taking off each other's clothes, I asked him if he had a condom. He said yes, laid me back on the bed, and placed his body gently on top of me. He looked deeply into my eyes and I'm sure I registered awe.

We both were in awe, truth be told. He was fulfilling a childhood dream, and I was amazed that a man who looked like him was enamored with me. I had never in my entire life had a man to focus on my body the way Marcus did that night.

What was even more amazing was how we had that kind of sex without waking up Terry, who was sleeping just a few feet from us in the other bed. Marcus had to cover my mouth with his hand at one point.

The next morning, all three of us went out for breakfast before Terry and I drove back to Milwaukee. Marcus kept pulling me close to him whenever Terry wasn't paying attention. He even laid his head on my shoulder.

He continued looking at me with puppy-dog eyes, as if he was already in love with me. As for me, I was still in shock. I could not believe I let that happen. There was no way I could be with Marcus. This is going to sound harsh; nonetheless, Marcus was a hood dude from the West Side of Chicago. I knew how this movie was going to play out, and no matter how I might try to rewrite the ending, a relationship with Marcus was not going to end well. I could not have someone like him in my young son's life. Now I just had to figure out how I was going to break the news to Marcus—while he continued to hold me close to him up to the moment Terry and I got into my car to drive away. He held my hand and asked me to promise to call him once I got back to Milwaukee.

Chapter 12

HEARTBREAKS

AFTER MY EPISODE WITH MARCUS, AJ AND I started going to church consistently. I was one of those "praising God on Sunday Christians" and lived how I wanted the rest of the week. I was quickly out the door once the services ended. I didn't talk about my faith with anyone other than my friend Elnora. I knew she went to church as well. You could not convince me that I wasn't a super Christian who loved God and walked with Him every day of my life.

For that reason, it was time to have the difficult talk with Marcus. I did not go into detail with him about how my beliefs were weighing on me and leading me to rethink the life choices I would make. I knew Marcus was not at a place in his life to understand where I was coming from. Like many individuals

I knew, he had an awareness of God; he even prayed from time to time.

Unlike some of my previous relationships, where I approached separations recklessly, I wanted to handle ending things with Marcus carefully. So instead of avoiding his calls, we had an open and honest conversation a few nights after the party. We talked about how much fun we had, especially our time at the hotel. We laughed and teased each other, but then Marcus turned serious, sharing how much he wanted to be my man.

The clear truth was that I was in my thirties, while Marcus was a twenty-three-year-old man with no plan for his future other than hustling in the streets of Chicago. I could not see him as my man. Marcus interjected, saying that he knew the type of man I wanted, and he was willing to be that man for me. If he was going to change his behavior, Marcus needed to change it for himself, not just to be with me.

I took a deep breath and proceeded with...the truth. I affirmed that I enjoyed our time together and appreciated how easily we could share our feelings. Marcus had become silent on the other end of the call. I continued by saying our behavior that night had been foolish. We had thrown caution to the wind, and despite how magical the night felt, I could not be that careless again. I ended the call by asking him to understand where I was coming from as the mother of a young son. I needed to set a better example for my son. Marcus said he understand but added that he would move to Milwaukee in a heartbeat if I were to change my mind.

A month later, I suspected that I might be pregnant. I'd been having baby urges around that time but was determined not to bring another child into the world unless I was married or at least had a partner who would be engaged with our child on a regular basis. Raising AJ without the support of Anton had been extremely difficult and exhausting for me; I never wanted to have that experience again.

I knew that the sadness of not having my own father in my life had left a hole in my heart that could not be filled—no child should know that heartbreak.

I called Marcus to ask what he would do if I were pregnant. If I were, he said, he'd be in Milwaukee that same night. Marcus didn't have children and he was excited. Regardless, my world was shaken. His enthusiasm made me even more terrified. If I was pregnant, did he think he was just going to move in with me?

Other questions quickly cluttered my mind. "What would the people at church think of me?" "What would the people at my job say about me?"

The following day, I decided to find out one way or the other if I was pregnant. While sitting in the waiting room of the walk-in clinic, I prayed to God for the results to be negative. I pleaded with Him not to punish me for something I did not intentionally do. I felt as though this time it was not my fault. I'd asked if he had a condom.

The nurse returned with a positive result. I was pregnant. There I was, supposedly living the life of a saved woman, going to church every week, only to be pregnant outside of wedlock. Again.

Sitting in my car, I yelled at God and pounded the roof with the palm of my hand. "I finally started trusting You, and this is what I get?" I decided in that moment I was going to get an abortion. I went straight home to call my friend Lakesha. Lakesha was another one of the dear friends that I had made while working at the Sheraton.

Once Lakesha answered the phone, I started crying and told her that I needed her to just be my friend and not to judge me for what I was about to share with her. Lakesha said that she would be there for me regardless of what I decided to do.

I found a clinic and made an appointment for the following week. When Marcus asked, I told him I wasn't pregnant, because I did not want both of us to have to deal with the guilt of my abortion. The only people who knew the truth about my pregnancy were Elnora and Lakesha.

Talking with Elnora by her desk, I asked her if she wanted to know a secret. I told her that I wanted the baby, but I couldn't keep him or her. She looked at me lovingly and said, "Jennifer, if you want to keep the baby, don't go through with the abortion." I tried to shush her, and told her to be quiet, even putting my left index finger to my lips. I was certain I would go through with the abortion. My soul still needed to say out loud that I wanted my baby—and to have someone else to hear and know it too.

On the day of my appointment, Lakesha and I went to the clinic. As we were walking up to the clinic, a woman with some brochures came up to me and tried to talk me out of getting the abortion by letting me know that there are people available who could help me with the baby. She also suggested that I consider letting someone adopt the baby. I wanted to pacify the lady by listening, but my mind was made up. I was convinced that I preferred to return my baby's spirit back to God rather than bring her or him into a world with parents who were not prepared to take care of a child. Unlike me, Lakesha was not listening to anything the lady had to say. When the woman placed the pamphlet in my hand, Lakesha took it and threw it on the ground towards the woman's feet.

After the procedure, the lady with the pamphlets went from being my counsel to my jury. "You will have to answer to God for what you have done," she called to me. Lakesha, without missing a beat, told the lady, "And so will you."

After the abortion, I decided that I would not have sex again unless I could see myself marrying the man that I was with. With that decision, I continued with my life as usual by going to church and work each week and hanging out with my family and friends when time permitted. AJ was twelve years old at this time, and he preferred hanging out with his cousins and Elnora's son Mott rather than being with me or going to church. Nonetheless, I still made him go with me to church each week.

Four months after the abortion had taken place, I received a call from a cousin in Chicago. She asked me to guess who had died. I thought she was going to say Larry because he had been battling cancer. When she said Marcus' name, I was quiet. I assumed she was talking about a different Marcus had gotten shot at a dice game. My world sank when she confirmed it was my Marcus and that the funeral was that day.

I let her know that I was on my way and dialed Terry immediately. He couldn't leave his job, so I left for Chicago without him. I dropped off AJ with my mom and called Lakesha from the road. I was sobbing angrily, choking on my words. I promised to drive carefully and pressed my way on to Chicago.

Arriving at his grandmother's house, I had to accept the truth that my Marcus was dead. Everywhere I looked, I saw people wearing white t-shirts with Marcus' face on it that read sunrise and sunset, denoting Marcus' birth and death. I continued to make my way through Marcus' grandmother's house, asking people where I could find Marcus' mother. Once I was able to reach her, I just gave her a big hug and told her that I was the sister of Terry, one of Marcus' friends from Milwaukee, who she knew as Chief.

"Oh, I know Chief," she said and asked if he was with me. I told her that he was not, and that I would let him know that she had asked about him. She offered me something to eat, but I declined, saying that I had to get back on the road soon.

I had to see for myself if it was true about Marcus. His mother shook her head in disbelief; she'd been in shock longer than I had, obviously. I did not ask any additional questions. I hugged her again and prepared to go.

As I left the house from the backyard and headed towards my car, I saw Marcus and Terry's other childhood friend, Arlee. We hugged, and I asked if he knew why anyone would want to kill Marcus. Arlee said he wasn't sure why it happened. I wasn't sure I believed him, so I just gave him another hug and told him to be careful and to take care of himself.

I felt different about Marcus' death than I did about my sister Chandra's death. With her, I felt cheated out of several opportunities for us to experience life together due to the decisions of other people that were out of our control. With Marcus, I just felt a lot of regret and "what ifs." What if I would have allowed our relationship to continue? What if I had been honest about being pregnant? What if I did not allow what others might think to supersede what I did want for myself? I was not in love with Marcus, but I did care about him a great deal. And more than anything, I had wanted him to be okay.

When I made it back to Milwaukee, I was emotionally drained. I picked up AJ from my mom at auntie Minnie Lee's house, and we went straight home to our apartment. For the rest of the night, only thing I had energy for was to lie on my couch and pray. I was not sure what to pray for, so I prayed to God and I told God that I needed for Marcus to be okay. I needed to know that Marcus had made it to heaven. After praying to God, I talked to Marcus. I told him that I needed to know that he was okay, and if he was okay, I wanted him to send me a penny from heaven.

The next morning, I drove to work as I normally did, and as I exited my car a penny rolled off me and dropped to the ground. I felt such relief that God and Marcus had both heard me and graciously let me know that Marcus was okay and with God in heaven.

My Marcus has been dead for well over fifteen years now, yet I still think of him every time I come across a penny on the ground. I see the pennies as his way of saying hello to me. The great thing about those pennies is that I come across one when I need cheering up. It does not happen often, but when it does, I collect the penny and place it in a vase.

The very first penny from heaven that rolled off me I taped to the letter that I wrote to Marcus after his death. I wrote the letter to him to say what I was not able to tell him when he was alive. In the letter, I thanked him for the magical night that we shared. I thanked him for the way he looked at me. I wanted Marcus to know how much I appreciated him wanting to be a better man for me. I also let him know how deeply I cared about him and how I wished we could have had more time with one another. Like every other situation in my life that I had no control over, I put away the letter, and I did my best not to allow Marcus' death to affect any other part of my life. I needed to move forward, and for me that meant moving forward with God.

Chapter
13

GOD'S GRACE

ONE OF MY MANY REGRETS IS THAT IT TOOK ME too long to get to know God for myself. I rejected Him as a young girl—not just because of the evil that happens in the world. I rejected Him because of the evil that happened to me. I wondered to myself, "What kind of God would allow me to be raped as a child? What kind of God would give me a mother that allowed herself to be repeatedly beaten by a man, a mother more concerned about her next drink than protecting her children?"

I resented my mom through much of my life until God allowed me to see her as a broken little girl as well—one who also suffered much loss and trauma. When I started praying to God, He got me to see that my mother did the best she could for me and my siblings. And if she could've given more, she would have.

God gave me the wisdom to begin showing my mother mercy instead of condemnation. I became more patient with her. I asked her questions about her life and what she thought about different things. I started seeing my mother as a woman, and not just my mother.

With prayer and by applying God's Word to my life, I was able to learn to honor my mother as God would have me. Instead of constantly being critical of her, I accepted her as the woman she was, and not some version I desired her to be. I realized that despite her faults, my mother did love me, and had she known any of those horrible things that happened to me occurred, she would have gone through hell to protect me. Moreover, she loves my son and would give him the shirt off her back and her last dollar.

When AJ was circumcised as a toddler and I couldn't stay home with him for the entire week as he recovered, who came over to my apartment to stay with him while I worked? My mother. When AJ needed assistance going to and from the bathroom after he got shot, who was there to help him? My mother.

I slowly was able to forgive my mother, even though she continued her drinking, I realized she showed me love in the way that I couldn't appreciate when I was younger. My mother was there when I needed her, and she celebrated me for each of my accomplishments even when she did not understand why I felt the need to achieve them.

Because I was raised in a dysfunctional home and an impoverished environment, I developed a mindset that mirrored dysfunction and poverty. In other words, I felt that I always had to be in survival mode in an effort not to go back there. However, instead of focusing on seeking that next educational degree, I pursued God's Word. The Bible told me to "Be anxious for nothing, but in everything by prayer and supplication, with thanksgiving let your requests be made known to God" (Philippians 1:6–7, KJV).

I continued my path of studying God's Word and applying it to my life. And whenever I was struggling with something, I would locate a Bible verse that applied to that situation, then seek revelation from God through prayer until I felt a breakthrough in my heart. Some verses that helped me were those that talked about forgiveness. Specifically, Jesus tells us, "For if you forgive other people when they sin against you, your heavenly Father will also forgive you. But if you do not forgive others their sins, your Father will not forgive your sins" (Matthew 6:14–15, NIV).

These Bible verses are some of the ones that made me say ouch instead of amen. I knew there was a lot of unforgiveness I needed to work through, especially for myself.

It seemed that whatever verse I was studying, all the pastors I watched on television would speak about that same subject. If I was studying forgiveness, Bishop Jakes and Pastors Osteen and Prince were preaching about forgiveness. I'd go to church, and Pastor Harvey would preach on forgiveness.

I intentionally worked to get the Word of God in me. The more of the Word I got in me, the more I started to get uncomfortable being in certain places and participating in certain behaviors.

Going to church on a Friday night became more fun than going to the bar. If the doors of the church were open, I was there. As I got closer to God, my friendships changed. I left the hospitality industry and moved into academia.

I wanted a career where I felt I could do some good and give back to others. Working with researchers and medical students at the medical institution helped me to fulfil that need for a time; however, a thought would arise and let me know there was more I could do. That led me to volunteering in my church.

I'd sign up to clean the streets, babysit in the nursery, go on prayer walks, be a teacher's aide for the toddlers, and finally I settled on assisting the cook in the church's café.

I thought I could volunteer my way to deserve God's forgiveness. Eventually I realized I did not have to work for what I already had. God forgave me the moment I gave up my own will and accepted His will for my life. God was not interested in what I might do for Him, He wanted me to be with Him so that He could introduce me to His Son Jesus.

As I got to know Jesus, I started to become overwhelmed by God's love for me. All the sadness, loneliness, and regret began to fall away from me because God loves me. The emptiness of not knowing my biological family was filled with the love from my heavenly father.

God had forgiven me for all my transgressions, and it was time for me to forgive myself. And I needed to learn to trust what God says about me in His Word as truth.

I looked to Jesus to be my example. When tempted by the devil, Jesus quoted Scripture. So I began posting verses from the Bible that I could stand on whenever I felt tempted. They were posted on my bathroom mirror, in my journal, on my desk.

In addition to the Word of God, what also helped me was I did not want to grieve the Holy Spirit. God had given me His Spirit as a comforter and counselor. By intentionally sinning, I was complicit in bringing about death. As according to Scripture, "Then, after desire has conceived, it gives birth to sin; and sin, when it is full-grown, gives birth to death" (James 1:15 NIV).

Even if it did not lead to physical death in some cases, God's Word has shown this to be true in my life. Therefore, instead of grieving the Holy Spirit I wanted to get to know God better and have His grace to shine down on me and through me.

To know God even more I incorporated fasting, prayer, and studying the Bible as part of my lifestyle.

While I was studying the Bible, Jesus came alive to me. It was a startling awakening that someone like me, someone who wasn't raised in the church could discover such an intimate relationship with God.

I found myself unhooking many shields and presumptions, opening myself wider to this profound and pure cleansing. From Genesis to Revelation, the Bible reads like a love letter from God.

As I learned more about the Bible, I decided to get baptized again. After my second baptism I felt what I did not feel the first time, which was being accepted and loved wholeheartedly. I was so overwhelmed with emotions that I wept the entire time up until I was dipped in the water—as I came up, I felt clarity and freedom.

God has always been with me. He says so in His Word: "Be strong and courageous. Do not be afraid or terrified because of them, for the Lord your God goes with you, He will never leave you or forsake you" (Deuteronomy 31:6, NIV).

That season of diligent study taught me how to dive into the pages of the Bible for tools, not just talking points. Because I trusted God, He led me to Jesus, and Jesus has given me a love beyond anything my heart has ever hoped for.

In one of my favorite passages Jesus said, "My prayer is not for them alone. I pray also for those who will believe in me through their message, that all of them may be one, Father, just as you are in me and I am in you. May they also be in us so that the world may believe that you have sent me. I have given them the glory that you gave me, that they may be one as we are one. I in them, and you in me so that they may be brought to complete unity. Then the world will know that you sent me and have loved them even as you have loved me" (John 17:20-23 NIV).

By finally accepting the love of Jesus, I was brought to my knees. He gave me the confidence I could not find in a textbook.

Regardless of my starting point, God loves me, and His love overwhelms me. I'm privileged to call Him my friend. Unlike others throughout my life, I never have to doubt God's love for me.

Whether we are new to Christianity or have walked with God for decades, it is essential to discover the root of our struggles to effectively face it, soften it, and pluck it free. I am a living testimony to God's goodness and grace, and His desire to make us whole, all of us.

God helped me name the emotions and decisions that later sprang from my abandonment, abuse, instability, and insecurities. His Word provided me the might and means to withstand the emotional weight and spiritual awakening that followed. The line that brought me the most comfort was the one Jesus said," I will not leave you as orphans, I will come to you" (John 14:18, NIV).

For that I am eternally grateful. Amen.

Chapter
14

REFLECTIONS AND NOTES

As I continuously lean on God's Word to become whole, I understand that my challenges do not end there. Being aware of my broken pieces allows me to trust God, full stop.

Here are some nuggets I would like to share with you as well:

- When opportunities do not come in the way you wanted them to, trust God.
- We often give more weight to what others think about us than what God's Word says about us. Let God's Word have the first and final say when it comes to what you think about yourself.
- Know that your body is a temple and that no one has the right to abuse it, not even you. It is critical to teach

this lesson to your children at an early age in a way that is appropriate for her or him.

- Manipulating others is not a good strategy for success.
- Everything you need is already within you—unlike what the widow declared to the prophet Elisha: "Your servant has nothing there at all, she said, except a small jar of olive oil" (2 King 4:2). Believe that God can and will use your "small anything" as a tool to bless you, your family, and others. The only thing He requires is your obedience.
- How your life story begins does not have to be how it ends.
- When changes happen in your life, and they will, start seeing them as opportunities for you to become an even greater version of yourself.
- Struggles come to strengthen you, not to break you.
- Forgive yourself for everything, then apply that same grace to others.
- God loves you. Repeat that as often as you need to until you believe it in your heart and soul. Let's practice it: "God loves me." Say it again, again, and again.
- When in doubt, turn to Jesus.
- Selah.

ACKNOWLEDGEMENTS

A sincere thank you to all of you who purchase my book and learn from my story.

A special thank you to my pastors and teachers, who poured into my life through their teachings. Moreover, I want to thank my family for instilling in me, despite it all, love and perseverance.

Thank you to Joyce Taylor Washington and Dasha Kelly Hamilton for providing the initial edits of my book and for supporting me throughout this process. I am forever indebted to you all!

Lastly, I want to thank God for His patience with me and the ultimate gift of His Son Jesus Christ.

Resources

Berry, John, director. *Claudine.* / produced by Third World Films, distributed by 20th Century Fox, 1974.

Side-by-Side Bible, NIV & KJV (Zondervan, 2011).

Hudlin, Reginald, director. *Boomerang.* / produced by Imagine Entertainment, distributed by Paramount Pictures, 1992.

Project Ujima

Ward family photo archives

Zemeckis, Robert, director. *Forrest Gump.* Produced by Wendy Finerman Production, distributed by Paramount Pictures, 1994.